decorating

kids'
rooms

and family-friendly
spaces

QUARRY

pages 18–29, 34–51, 60–71, 82–103, 164–193, 236–265 © 2001 Anna Kasabian

pages 1–17, 30–33, 53–59, 72–81, 104–163, 194–235, 266–272 © 2004 by Quarry Books

First published in the United States of America by:
Quarry Books, an imprint of
Rockport Publishers, Inc.
33 Commercial Street
Gloucester, Massachusetts 01930-5089
Telephone: (978) 282-9590
Fax: (978) 283-2742
www.rockpub.com

Library of Congress Cataloging-in-Publication Data

ISBN 1-59253-094-X
10 9 8 7 6 5 4 3 2 1

Cover Images: Kevin Thomas, top left and bottom right; John Hall, top right; Paul Whicheloe, bottom left

Grateful acknowledgment is given to Lynne Farris for her work from *Baby Crafts* on pages 52–55; to Anna Kasabian for her work from *Kids' Rooms* on pages 18–29, 34–51, 60–71, 82–103, 164–193, and 236–265; to Sandra Salamony for her work from *Hand Lettering for Crafts* on pages 56–59; and to Eugenia Santiesteban for her work from *Living with Kids* on pages 8–17, 30–33, 72–81, 104–163, and 194–235.

Printed in China

decorating

kids' rooms

and family-friendly
spaces

Anna Kasabian and Eugenia Santiesteban

GLOUCESTER MASSACHUSETTS

QUARRY BOOKS

contents

introduction

If you have ever lived with children, you are well aware of the constant state of disarray and how quickly a very organized world is turned upside down. Although it is nearly impossible to change this dynamic, it is possible to design your family space to enhance and accommodate the creative disarray that seems to follow children wherever they go.

Decorating Kids Rooms and Family-Friendly Spaces was created to provide you with the resources, inspiration, and tools you need to create a livable and beautiful space that allows you to live in harmony as grown-ups and children.

This book helps you create a home that not only looks good but that grows with your family by including great design ideas from expert designers for creating everything from kid's bedrooms to family rooms that accommodate kid's birthday parties as well as dinner parties.

As you begin to consider the design of your child's room and the family spaces in your home, think first about what you want your house to be and the job you need it to do. Plan for whatever this is—comfort, energy, togetherness, safety, privacy, creativity, or family interaction.

Let your kids be involved in the design decisions, especially for their own private spaces. This allows them to appreciate the space and to feel ownership.

Storage and privacy are two elements that should not be overlooked in a family house. Storage is an essential consideration for an organized family-friendly space and should be worked in wherever possible. Private space, like storage, will reduce the tension and chaos associated with living with a group of individual personalities.

The most important thing to remember when planning the design of your family home is that you are a unit as a family but you are also all individual personalities with different needs. The most livable design is one that takes these varying needs into consideration. Just be careful not to make it too comfortable or your kids will never move out!

ground rules for family-friendly design

As you proceed, it is helpful to keep certain guidelines in mind. For example, choose furniture that you not only love but that is also practical. Always try to buy well-made furniture: It will better stand up to heavy use and perhaps even become an heirloom that you pass on to your child. Sturdier woods such as oak and mahogany are less ubiquitous than they used to be, but they'll last a lifetime. Well-constructed pine or other lighter woods can serve just as well.

Furniture commonly outlasts its original use and usually can be reassigned elsewhere or adapted to fit a family's changing needs, so buy with long-term plans in mind. If you buy things you really love, you'll be more likely to want to use them again and again. Remember: Growing children have quickly changing needs, which means frequent rearranging of furniture from room to room.

Designing kid-friendly spaces might also mean shrinking away from placing delicate family heirlooms in high-traffic areas like the living room; these pieces can be reassigned as well. Your great aunt's Wedgwood vase might really look great in the guest room. Don't hide away all your antiques though, especially the less-delicate ones. It's never too early to teach children to be respectful of possessions.

Organization and appropriate storage are key. Families accumulate clutter. Your home will look and work better if you figure out where and when the clutter accumulates, and design your home so that intercepting it is easier. Cubbies for soccer cleats in the mudroom, a rack for kids' computer game discs in the office by the computer—coming up with creative solutions is better than forever picking up the piles.

Remember that inspiration can come from anywhere. Be sure to keep yourself open to ideas you might incorporate into your decorating scheme. Whether it's a bedroom layout spotted at your next-door neighbors' home, or the cerulean blue of the ceiling at Grand Central Station, all is fodder for decorating. Don't discriminate; just remember those ideas that appeal to you and apply them in your space. You'll be surprised at the end result.

GETTING started

Now that you've decided to redo your home, the first step is outlining your goals. Whether you're planning a complete renovation, or just some minor streamlining and beautifying, writing your ideas down will help you get organized. Start with a comprehensive wish list. Write down everything you'd like to do, and then prioritize. Which things on your list are most important and most achievable? Do a little research at this point. What do things really cost? Talk to friends who have survived renovations or whose homes you admire, and ask them what works and what doesn't. Think about the alternatives: Can you paint or resurface your existing kitchen cupboards, or are new ones necessary?

Once you've decided on the targets and goals of your project, go over your plans with all the members of your family. Asking for help and ideas is a great way to get kids involved in a project. After all, everyone in the household should have a say, and if it's something directly involving their lives and day-to-day routine, you'll be surprised at how much input children will want to add!

OPPOSITE Before you start any redesign of your home, gather the family to discuss their needs and preferences so you can design a home that accommodates everyone. Conversation, board games, television, or video games can take place simultaneously in this family's living room.

the budget

Once everyone in the family has approved the overall plan, the next step is creating a budget and an action plan. Depending on the size of your renovation, the money that you'll need to set aside for your project will differ greatly. If you plan on making major changes, it may be helpful to get professional estimates. If so, obtain quotes from at least a few different professionals to ensure that you're getting a fair price. Estimates can vary widely. Use a spreadsheet to get organized and put all budget information in one easily accessible place.

Consider Your Timetable

Next, make a list of the rooms that you want to make less-extensive changes to. Estimate the costs for each, including paint jobs, furniture, storage systems, and accessories. If replacing furniture is too costly, new slipcovers, upholstery, or even new bedding can completely change the look of a room without the hefty price tag. It's also important to make a long-term plan. How long will the changes that you make need to last? Are you in a rental apartment and planning to move within a few years, or are you in a house and expecting to live there for decades? Whether your budget is limited, or you want to plan for the long haul, trendy options are better left to accessories and smaller objects than to large pieces of furniture. Versatility can be key in such cases.

Once you've talked to the contractors or workmen you'll need to hire, you should discuss the renovation schedule with the rest of the family. Maybe it's best to work on the children's rooms over the summer while they're away at camp or busy with summer activities, rather than in the fall when they're just getting back into school. Or perhaps fall is a good time to work on the living room when everyone is gone much of the day because of work or school. Decide what works best for you and your family and try to come up with a realistic time frame.

Remember that it isn't necessary to get everything done all at once, especially when buying expensive pieces of furniture. Even for renovation, accomplishing a little bit at a time over a longer time span might be better if you're making costly changes. Or perhaps if the budget isn't an issue, you'd like to get the work done or make all purchases you need as quickly as possible to disrupt your family as little as possible. Decorating is never really done. Improvements can always be made, but the key is to stick to your budget and know when to stop. Otherwise, your finances can easily spiral out of control.

picking a design aesthetic

Next, get inspired! Rip pages that you like out of magazines or catalogs. If you admire a home or a room that you've seen, jot down notes about it. Collect swatches of fabric that catch your eye, or paint-color chips that you're considering. As with anything, inspiration can come from anywhere—a decorating magazine, the lighting in a museum, or a display window that catches your eye as you walk down the street. And never be afraid to borrow. If a room you've been in feels comfortable, it's perfectly acceptable to mimic the layout or color scheme in your own home. Start keeping a folder with all the ideas you collect. It will be a reference when you're feeling stuck, and a place to gather your inspirations. You'll be surprised at how many images and samples you collect—and you'll be gratified when you look back and see how you translated those ideas into reality.

It is helpful at this point to narrow down your style preferences. Look at your favorite rooms and try to figure out which style category they fall into: classic American colonial, French country, modern, fifties retro, Swedish country—almost any look can be translated into a comfortable, beautiful family home. It's OK to be eclectic too, but it's better to mix and match on purpose than by accident. Serendipity notwithstanding, you'll save time and effort if you focus your search before you start.

Use What You've Got

Location often decides decorating needs as well. How much light does the room get, and which way does it face? Does it have a view—of a lake, ocean, rugged mountains, or city rooftops—that you want to emphasize? If the house is in a city, should you soundproof the baby's room? Who will use rooms the most, and for what purposes? All these factors should influence your decisions. Consider the design elements you already have in the house, especially architectural details. High ceilings give a wonderfully majestic feel to a room, besides providing an amazing backdrop for art. Existing fireplaces, mantelpieces, or columns have an air of built-in *gravitas*. Beams, moldings, and other structures can give character to a room. If details such as these aren't already in your home, some of them can be added or mimicked. For example, wainscoting is fairly easy to add to a bedroom or bathroom and it lends an old-fashioned, country feeling to a room. Your interior decoration doesn't have to conform to the style of your house, but considering its architecture beforehand will help define what you need to do.

Choose the Right Paint

The color of a room also influences the decor. A good way to decide which colors you want is to buy several options in a tester size; many paint companies sell small vials for such a purpose. Paint poster boards with the different hues and hang them up on the wall in the room you'll be painting. The nuances in paint formulas are surprisingly different from one another, as is the way in which colors look in a specific room, depending on the quantity and quality of light the room gets.

OPPOSITE Never underestimate the power of color to transform a room. Set off a strong shade, like that of these walls and bed, against a stark white background—linens and woodwork in this case—for an effect that's pure magic.

input from the family

Don't forget about who will be living in the rooms. Including children in the planning process not only helps them feel invested in the outcome but also provides refreshing ideas that reflect the children's personalities, and gives them an opportunity to mark their own territory, especially in their bedrooms. Set boundaries, however. Your children may want to poster their room with magazine pages, or hope to have a tent in the middle of the room for a bed, but that doesn't mean you're obliged to comply. (It's never too early to teach them the value of practicality!) As long as you allow them a voice in making choices, they'll feel more in control of their space. If, for example, you're set on buying a particular bed for your child, let the child choose the bedding. Even if you don't love the choices the child makes, you can repaint and redecorate the room later. In the end, the important thing is that your child will remember that you listened.

survival tips

Although planning a renovation project can be fun if you involve your children, in reality, it can be long and complicated and create lots of tension within a family. The schedule lags behind, expenses multiply, and differences can become a source of struggle. Understand that problems can arise, and be prepared to deal with them as they come.

If you're on a strict schedule—for example, renovating a bedroom to prepare for a new baby—have a backup plan in case something goes awry. Maybe another room in the house, or even a cradle in the master bedroom, can serve as a temporary nursery until the real room is ready. A renovation is an evolving, constantly changing process. You may run into construction snags that you couldn't have foreseen, or you may find yourself changing your mind a few times during the process, or not liking something once it's done. It's always better to try and change something you don't love at the initial stages rather than five years down the road.

Before construction starts, have a conversation with your family, letting them know how long you expect the process to take, as well as the extent of the changes. Ask for their patience and cooperation. If sacrifices must be made, try to help the children remember that maturity is appreciated, and that the long-term result will be worth waiting for. Remind yourself that the whole point of the renovation is to make a more relaxed, comfortable home for your family.

OPPOSITE Work together with your child to arrive at a compromise. Maybe putting toys on the kitchen floor isn't the best idea, but don't rule it out before you give it a try! If your floor is less spacious than this, perhaps a bin for crayons, paper, and scissors on the kitchen table can provide another way to bring toys into the kitchen.

Making Room

INFANTS

The best way to develop a design plan for an infant's room is to think through the big picture of your family life. Is this room likely to be used by the same child for several years, or will it always be the new baby's room?

If your family is growing and this is the first of several children you plan to have, consider designating it the infant's room. This way, you need to decorate and furnish it only once for at least a few years. For flexibility, choose yellow as a main color, and keep decorations themed to accommodate both boys and girls.

You will spend a lot of time in your baby's room, so in planning it, take into account your activities, style of organization, and the everyday needs of babies. Infants use bedrooms mainly for sleeping and having diapers and outfits changed. You'll be going in and out of here a lot, tending to these tasks, so storage, lighting, and flooring must be carefully considered.

If possible, choose a room that is not too far from your bedroom so that late-night feedings and diaper changes can be attended to quickly without disrupting the rest of the family. Also, you'll be glad not to run down a long hall or climb stairs when you've just woken up.

In addition, if you've got the luxury of space, choose a room away from where your toddlers sleep. A new baby's fussing can be disruptive.

This chapter on infants' rooms will help you think through design options and offer tips on choosing a theme and accessorizing.

Opposite: Remember how much time you will spend here when you select wallpaper and furnishings. This room's soft, subtle floral wallpaper will not get stale, and it's set up with pleasing reminders that your daughter will soon be at the table playing! Notice the rocker; you will want one for late-night feedings.

Above: Create a fantasy room for yourself and your baby. Here, a soft mint green pastel dominates, and a decorative wall painting suggests a forest. The trees and animals on the walls are accented with bunting and a little painted table; both express the nature theme.

How to Choose a Theme

Before making any design decisions, consider whether or not this room will remain the new baby room. If it will, you should definitely invest in well-made, sturdy furnishings rather than trendy, less durable styles. Likewise, select a theme that will endure, be suitable for both boys and girls, and be pleasing to you. After all, you will be in and out of this room, day and night, for many months.

On the other hand, if this will remain your child's room for several years, choose design options that can easily make the transition from infant to toddler to perhaps a seven-year-old with minimal expense.

Ask yourself these questions:

• What kind of chair would be best for rocking the baby?
• When I greet the baby in the morning, sun streaming through the windows, what colors and patterns will make me feel happy?
• What can be added to the walls and floors for me and the baby to talk about?

Many design choices are available. To come to the right decision, think about themes in broad terms:

• **Fantasy:** This kind of room takes you to a new place and time. It may have nothing to do with the rest of the home's decor. The crib may be surrounded with a tent of fabric, ribbons, and bows, for example, and may remind you of a romantic story you read once. Practicality is not in this room plan!
• **Ultramodern:** This room takes advantage of all that is sleek, clean, and contemporary. Furnishings have simple lines and the palette is in subtle shades of white, off-white, and cream. Carry the theme to the walls and adorn them with black-and-white photographs framed simply in black or white wood. Wallpaper might be simple—perhaps elegant angel wings that accent one wall or a portion of a wall.

Above: Notice how the bunnies and other little creatures carry onto the lampshade, soaps, and other decorative items. These little setups are nice and soothing for both you and your baby to look at.

Opposite: Take a traditional design path and use wallpaper with a storybook theme. This approach allows easy accessorizing. Also, with all-white furniture and window treatments, other fabrics can be introduced that hold to the palette.

- **Antique:** Taking this route offers lots of design possibilities and period themes, from colonial to French country to Victorian. Bureaus, chairs, and armoires can anchor the theme, and accessories like antique photos, floor lamps, and quilts enhance it. Follow through with wall paint as well as wallpaper. Many companies reproduce period colors and patterns.
- **Traditional:** Visuals like storybook characters, farmyard scenes, or children at play make their way into these rooms via fabric, wallpaper, rugs, hand-painted furniture, and even lampshades. Furniture styles that work nicely here vary from white woods to naturals.

The next job is to think about how to incorporate a theme. The possibilities are myriad. Keep in mind the length of time the room will be used by the child—infancy only or on through toddlerhood. Here are some options for versatile, budget-conscious design:

- Use a washable wallpaper pattern to introduce lots of pattern. For a nature theme with puppies or kittens, mix and match the paper with complementary colors. This is appropriate in both bedroom and bath.
- Try decorative painting on the walls, ceilings, or floors—or both. A storybook theme on the curtains could be reinforced by continuing a visual via paint.
- Express the theme on only the window treatments for easy changing.
- Cover only the ceiling in wallpaper! Sky patterned wallpaper makes a dreamy effect.
- Carry over visual themes in blankets, bunting, pillows, and upholstered furniture.
- Complement a theme with painted furniture. Bookcases, a table and chairs, and toy chests are all good candidates.

Above: Neutral walls and striped wallpaper with a subtle theme make it easy to alter this room when baby grows into boy. For the baby, the bunting carries the visual theme of knights; curtains in the same design will work fine for the toddler.

- Paint the upper portion of walls of the room and use themed wall-paper on the lower half. This makes changing the theme easier.
- Paint the walls a plain pastel color. Add an artistic pattern or mural to the ceiling.
- Use complementary colors on the walls and window borders. Introduce themes only on fabrics.
- Use wallpaper with stripes or another geometric form. Suggest that this is a baby's or young child's room with accessories like stuffed animals and hanging quilts.
- Use plain, checked, or striped fabric to frame windows; use hooks to drape it over each side of the window. To save money, buy one piece of fabric and hem it yourself with sewing tape. For an elegant look, buy extra fabric and let it pool on the floor. Use shades to darken the room. When it's time for a change, use the fabric to cover pillows or make a playroom tent.
- Use any fabric theme on a window shade to keep the decor very flexible and easy to change.
- Keep walls and curtains white. Introduce color and themes in the accessories.
- Choose a broad theme that's easy to live with, like the sky, or a simple theme, like the outdoors or the beach, that can repeat in interesting ways.

Whether you decide to paint the walls, use wallpaper, or do a little of both, remember that you want to step into this room and feel relaxed (even if you're not!), and you want your baby to feel soothed as well. The idea here is to avoid overstimulation. That's not to say scenes of children playing outside should be avoided, but it might be a good idea to investigate wallpaper scenes that look like soft watercolor creations.

Themes and Places to Carry Them Out

Consider choosing simple white or natural wood cribs and bureaus for the greatest freedom to work a theme, build a palette, and use the most options in fabric patterns. If you have family heirloom furnishings, don't worry about mixing eras. An antique bureau that belonged to your great-grandmother can work beautifully with a simple wooden crib. Use old family pieces, from your grandfather's train set to your mom's high chair as design elements. They'll provide eye-catching pools of history—things you can talk to your child about someday.

Here are some ways to weave a theme through your baby's room if antiques are the focus (many of these suggestions pertain to new items as well):

- Frame old postcards that align with the theme, and cluster ten or so on a wall.
- Line up antique toys, from fire engines to dolls, on a single shelf that surrounds the room.
- Hang an antique quilt that shares the palette or theme on the wall.
- Display antique children's clothing and other interesting pieces on the walls on antique hangers.

If the theme is babies at the beach, consider these options:

- Devote a portion of a wall to a display of toddler-size sand buckets and shovels.
- Paint the floor of the room to look like water and sand. Paper the lower half of the walls with colorful fish.
- Create a beach-themed lampshade by gluing shells around the edge of a plain shade.
- Use fabric that depicts a beach theme, or keep it simple and go with soft, pastel-striped cotton for curtains and pillows.

Above: There are many ways to bring a theme together. In this room, the teddy bear is repeated on the quilt, sleepwear bag, curtains, and a portion of the wallpaper. Since the major part of the wallpaper has flowers, butterflies, and geometric shapes, the theme can be changed easily and inexpensively.

Above: Consider putting antique heirlooms into your baby's room. The exquisite details on this marble-topped Victorian chest of drawers really stand out in the nearly all-white room. The blue-and-white hand-painted blocks on the hardwood floor also help the chest stand out and complement the other touches of blue.

Right: The curtain detailing adds a nice touch.

Above: Here's a good idea for a little girl's room. Use striped wallpaper and border it with the alphabet. This is a theme with staying power.

Supporting Accessories

The basics are discussed above. Enhance the theme by introducing accessories in the same palette or with complementary pictures. Here is a checklist of possibilities:

- stuffed animals
- posters (antique or new)
- clothing racks
- rugs
- clothing bags
- hampers
- lamps
- prints

- bookends
- night-lights
- toy chests
- clocks
- books
- photos
- paintings

Above: Here is an inexpensive way to accessorize using colorful wall art, stuffed animals, and a few standing sculptures. Changing this room from a baby's to a four-year-old's would require neither papering nor painting.

Left: Ready-made patterns can be matched with ease; many retailers offer coordinated linens and curtains, fabric, wallpaper, and quilts.

a growing nursery

Rapidly growing children present a decorating challenge. Pint-size proportions are quickly outgrown as a 2-year-old sprouts into a lanky 12-year-old. Try to create a room that will grow with your child, and seek out furniture that can transform and change, too. A bunk bed that convert into twin beds, a trundle bed that converts to extra storage, or a changing table that becomes a regular dresser can save space as well as money, and are wonderful pieces of furniture for growing children.

Keep It Simple

In a nursery, furnishings must be versatile enough to keep up with the rate of growth. A crib is quickly replaced with a child-size junior bed, which in turn is substituted by a full-size adult one. How do you accommodate a room whose furniture changes at the blink of an eye? Keep it simple, relaxed, and easily alterable.

If you're converting a spare room into a nursery and don't know the coming baby's sex, or if you're planning to use the room as a nursery for every subsequent member of your expanding clan, it's best to keep the main features neutral. White or neutral shades of wood and creamy-colored linens are the way to go. You can still use color, but do so sparingly and don't make it gender-specific. Primary colors are also a great backdrop. At first babies see black and white best, and then they see bright primary colors. Any shade of red, blue, or yellow is stimulating to an infant and is child-friendly enough to change later into either a girl's or boy's bedroom. Look for cribs that convert into junior beds, by removing the side rails, adding extensions, and adjusting the height. And when your toddler outgrows that bed, it can be used as a small sofa or daybed.

OPPOSITE A romantic crib can beautify a nursery without making it stuffy. Cover walls with neutral shades like these so that a nursery can transform into a child's bedroom or a grown-up sitting area.

Remember to Think Long Term

If the nursery has already been designated to grow along with your newborn, you can add some flavor. A girl's room can be covered in feminine wallpaper, and a boy's room can be done up in stripes. Think long term, though. Will a 10-year-old be just as comfortable with their nursery room's wallpaper? Decorate so that once the crib is dismantled, the nursery can grow with its occupant. Bunnies and ducks are cute, but even a 4-year-old will think that they're too infantile after awhile. Add touches like nursery-book illustrations on the walls, or shelves stocked with toys to announce that it's a baby's room. If you really don't like anything too cutesy, try brightly colored prints by artists such as Miró or Matisse, which can look great in a child's room.

Decorate for the Parents, Too

Make sure the nursery has at least one comfortable armchair. Parents will spend just as much time in this room as a newborn, and it's important to have a chair to sink into, whether it's for the 2 A.M. feeding or the 150th reading of *Good Night Moon*. A sofa or armchair with comfortable blankets at hand will do the trick. Shelves with baskets are a good way to keep clean towels, diapers, and other essentials at the ready in the nursery. Fabric-lined wicker keeps linens dry and clean. Also, don't forget a hamper for wet towels and clothes, a sturdy changing table, and a trash basket for easy disposal.

STYLE FILE: creative expression

Whether sleeping, doing homework, or simply relaxing, children should feel that their room reflects their true self. Let your children express themselves. If they can't find sheets in the exact purple they want, give them a set of white-jersey sheets and let them try to get it right with dye. Better yet, let them create their own sheets with fabric paint or tie-dye. Perhaps they'll want their friends to sign their sheets in color markers. Anything goes.

Another way to let creativity reign is by creating an art wall or board. Buy standard corkboard or a premade bulletin board from a supply store. Help children cover it with fabric, paint the border, add a ribbon detail, and cover it with a collage of ticket stubs, artwork, or photographs. Let them imbue it with their own style and interests, whether their mania is sports, animals, or skateboarding. Display the board above a desk or work area so that their own creativity can inspire them. A pretty option is to crisscross the board with ribbons so that pictures and reminders can be tucked underneath. An art wall is also a possibility. Hang drawings not just on the refrigerator door but in the bedroom as well. Standard art paper-sized frames can be bought at framing stores. Buy a number of frames and hang them together to create a rotating art gallery of your child's work. Children are proud to see their artwork on display.

Even in the most tailored of rooms, the tiniest details that children contribute will give any room flair and a sense of individual style. Always make an allowance for a creative touch that comes from your child.

EXPRESS YOURSELF

- Give your child a blank canvas in some shape or form for self-expression.
- Allow your child to make something for his or her room—for example, a drawing or some other artwork.
- A room should reflect a child's interests; add personal touches like equestrian prints or sports memorabilia.
- Encourage your child to hang photographs or artwork on a message board.
- Make an art wall that's entirely your child's domain.
- Even toddlers are creative; hang their drawings in their rooms, too.

UNEXPECTED **DECORATING IDEAS**

Design themes come in many forms, and they certainly do not have to be composed of the usual elements we know all too well. Here are fresh ideas for thinking outside the "design box."

Introduce a mommy tree on the wall. Incorporate as many **photographs of mommies** as you can find. Frame them in different-colored frames, or purchase unpainted frames and make decorating them a family project.

Sprinkle **mirrors** of different sizes and shapes around your baby's room. These are not only decorative but handy for pointing, talking, and distracting, when necessary.

Use **music boxes and music** as a **theme.** For example, antique or new music boxes can play sweet lullabies on your baby's bookshelves while you maintain the music theme with wallpaper or decorative painting (put multicolored notes all around the room or paint the words to a lullaby on the floor). Frame old or new music sheets of classic baby songs.

Go to flea markets and generate a small collection of baby dishes. Display them on shelves or hang them on the walls. Create a mobile with old **silver** baby feeding **spoons** and hang it near a window. When the breeze comes by, the spoons will ring.

A **PARENT** CORNER

Create a little corner for yourself in your baby's room, as a survival kits of sorts. When the baby is ill or fussy and alert to your presence in the room, a parent corner makes it easier for you to rock and read at the same time. Then, when the baby calms down and silence sets in, the quiet will let you relax a little, too.

For example, if you have a **rocker** in your baby's room, add a **side table** stocked with reading materials for yourself. If space permits, include a little **footstool** so you can rest, too.

Here are **other items** to consider leaving in a parent corner:

• an extra pair of reading glasses
• a book of poetry, a novel, magazines
• a reading light
• a little sewing or knitting project
• stationery and a pen
• loose photos and an album

Don't be caught by surprise; make a budget for your baby's room.

Do some homework so your design budget is realistic. Look through flyers and magazines, search furnishing sites on the Internet, and check costs for cribs, bedding, lamps, accessories, paint, and wallpaper.

If this task seems overwhelming, consider hiring an interior designer for an hourly fee to help develop a budget and make suggestions. Should you choose to do this on your own, make a list of mandatory furnishings—for example, crib, changing table, and rocking chair. Estimate their cost based on your research. Subtract that from the budget and see what's left for wallpaper, paint, carpeting, window treatments, and accessories like lamps, bookshelves, and incidental furnishings.

DECORATING **TIPS FROM A PRO**

Esther Sadowsky of Charm & Whimsy, Manhatten, New York, is an interior designer specializing in creating murals and custom-designed furniture for children's rooms. She designs everything from beds to lamps. Following are her tips on how to design and think about your child's space.

Make an **overall plan** before you buy: Clip photos of rooms, accessories, and color palettes that appeal to you; get samples from a fabric store; measure the dimensions of the room, including doors and windows; know your budget.

Think about how to **allocate the budget.** Would you prefer to spend more on wallpaper than carpeting? Fabric than wallpaper? This exercise is valuable whether you work with a designer or not.

If the budget is tight but you would like some help, work with a **retail store** to outfit your child's room.

Purchase extra fabric so as the room changes, you can **use the old theme in new ways**—to cover a comforter, for example. You can get the same fabric later, but it won't match perfectly.

Dry-clean fabrics for less fading. Dry-clean fabrics together for even treatment.

Remember that carpet fades over time. Think about this when you **place the crib,** which will eventually be replaced by the bed.

Allow some **space for play** and **creativity,** and include blackboards and bulletin boards.

To **avoid worry about spills and stains,** consider a few vinyl furniture coverings. Successful examples include window seat cushions and diaper changing pads. For rugs, use a fiber seal.

Consider a **flat-weave carpet** so toy trucks and cars can roll easily and puzzles can be assembled. Avoid sisal—too rough on the skin!

A bare floor is cold for kids. When you run in at midnight, you will appreciate **carpeting,** too.

Flexible lighting is important. Table lamps are fine, but if you're renovating, put sconces over the crib on a dimmer so you can feed the baby in the middle of the night.

Here are ideas for bringing elements of Samantha's drawing into a room design project:

- Line a windowsill with a small collection of miniature stuffed animals.

- Hunt for wallpapers, wallpaper borders, and accessories like lampshades, bed covers, curtains, and rugs with an animal theme.

- Note the colors in the drawing and see how they might work in the room. A solid hot-pink rug on a painted yellow floor could make for an exhilarating roomscape!

- Explore other ways to bring the stuffed animal theme into the room—perhaps a rug shaped like an animal. For example, Samantha has a white throw rug in her sitting room that resembles a dog.

Samantha

When I asked Samantha what her favorite part of her room was, she barely hesitated before choosing her stuffed animals. Here she drew one of her favorites, and she surrounded it with two others, just to make her design point! She held true to the colors and shapes that make up the stuffed animals, too.

Jennifer

I asked ten-year-old Jennifer to draw what she would like for wallpaper in her room, and she came up with this. Posing this question to your child can give you a good idea of what colors and shapes appeal and can jump-start a face-lift plan. I want to emphasize that this exercise can be offered as an idea for fun—not an absolute guarantee that the drawing will become the wallpaper.

"I want to **paint the walls** a dark color, have a **smiley-face border** in wallpaper, and then a **silver trim** that looks red one way and silver the other. I'd like a **bedspread** the same as the wall. The walls would have band **posters** on them."   —Jennifer, age 10

Here are ways to translate Jennifer's lead drawing into a room design. Note that purple is the color of choice, so if you think it can work, explore ways to weave it into the room or make it the predominant color.

Paint the walls pale lavender and the trim in a deeper purple. The darker color could work perfectly in an easy-to-clean, semigloss latex finish. Alternatively, paint the ceiling deep purple.

Find existing accessories that feature the smiley face—rugs, lampshades, etc.

Adapt the design idea to window treatments that you and your daughter make together. Sew a purple curtain and have your child cut smiley faces from yellow fabric and eyes and smiles from black. Sew the faces onto a band of fabric and sew the band to the purple curtain.

Develop a room with these colors as the base, and use the smiley faces as a pillow treatment. Buy pillows and make your own smiley face covers— you've taken the idea to a new place.

Nicole

Nicole is Jennifer's younger sister. The six-year-old decided to develop wallpaper with a sports theme. If her mom liked this idea, she could start a new room design by exploring existing wallpapers and fabrics that focus on sports—to see if any would work in Nicole's room.

Here are some ideas for incorporating Nicole's ideas into the design of her room:

Because Nicole is a young girl whose interests may change quickly, covering part of a wall in her room with blackboard would be an appealing, flexible way to encourage her creativity. She can then change her "wallpaper" whenever she wishes.

A good range of colors is presented here—from orange and pink to brown and green. Consider using green on the floor, through either carpet or paint, to bring the playing field inside.

Sports equipment could be stored in woven baskets, in a sports net hung on the wall, or on shelving. Nicole's parents could paint unfinished shelves with her favorite colors (they can always be repainted!) and add sports-themed decoupage to the shelves and edges.

Sheets, blankets, and curtain fabric can also be introduced with a sports theme.

"I would paint the walls a **darkish blue** and have a border with **sports** stuff. I like bunk beds because I'll be able to reach my radio. I'll keep my Pooh Bear sheets, but I'd like to put sticky **stars on the ceiling,** and I would like to plant two sunflowers, too."

—Nicole, age 6

My teddy bear

Marcella

Nine-year-old Marcella quickly drew three things that matter to her. She produced a big yellow pillow with her initial on it, her teddy bear, and a wallpaper pattern that she would love in her room.

Marcella's wallpaper pattern could be easily accomplished with a wall of blue paper and a border of little flowers. This could work in the bedroom and in a bathroom as well, if she has her own. The flowers could become part of a bigger theme and touch her linens, blanket, rugs, or wall art.

Here are some ways to interpret Marcella's designs and items:

- The yellow-and-red pillow and the teddy bear with a hint of red on his ears suggest a soft and cuddly theme to carry out via piles of pillows on the bed and, perhaps, a chair.

- The monogram could become a design element. Marcella could learn to sew and monogram items in the room herself. Kits are available to help with this. Parent and child could enjoy sharing this hobby.

- The teddy bear suggests a bear or broader animal theme. The latter could evolve into a circus theme, opening the possibility of faux painting or floor painting design projects.

- Continue the animal theme by covering a number of pillows with different fabrics printed with bears, elephants, leopard patterns, or jungle scenes.

AT LILI BAO LAN'S HOUSE

What makes a perfect room for kids is far from an exact science. For real-life answers to creating kid-friendly design with style and savvy—I turned to four families for ideas and inspiration. You'll find them profiled here, and through the rest of the book. Although no two children are the same, and each family has a completely unique background and approach, I hope that their collective creativity will give you rich possibilities for making kid smart designs of your own.

At 16 months, LiLi Bao Lan has taken over major portions of her old country cottage home, but the parents of this ever-smiling baby—whose name means precious orchard—don't mind one bit. Their house has trails of toys and books from the living room to the kitchen. Even in the dining room, a chandelier detailed with hanging bunny eggs makes a clever distraction on the walk to the breakfast table.

Of course, simple safety alterations have made the home more LiLi-friendly, but perhaps the best alteration is her parents thoughtful approach to decor that embraces their little girl's presence in every room. The living room—a grouping of comfortable seats—is pushed back, out of this en-ergized baby's path; her toys are here and there, ready for her hand or in-quisitive eye's focus. At this age, too, the need for multiple distractions is obvi-ous, so the room is well stocked!

Fireplace pokers are hidden behind chairs; table lamps are retired and small decorative accessories are stored away. Lili's mom, Katherine, decided to leave photos out, however, so that as LiLi moves about, she can play Who's That? with her parents.

In the kitchen, the silver items and plat-ters that once added color to the open

shelves were replaced with LiLi's drinking cup and toys. Under the work island is more LiLi turf—a big basket filled with plastic eggs and a whisk so she can pretend to help cook.

LiLi's bedroom walls are painted a soft, soothing blue-gray and green with a polka-dot pattern. The sheer curtains in the two sunny windows have pockets designed into them—the perfect solution for bedtime blues, as LiLi can listen to stories about the stuffed animals tucked into the pockets.

Other basic design elements include a crib, a bureau (which belonged to her grandparents and was painted white to match the crib), a changing table (with drawers that hold not only skin essentials but also toys to distract her while she's being changed), a rocking chair (a consignment shop find), and bookshelves, which are conveniently tucked behind the chair.

For safety's sake, hard, unbreakable toys are on the lower shelves, surrounded by soft stuffed animals. Books are stored higher so LiLi cannot pull them down, but when she's in the rocker with Mom, she can see the books and choose the day's reading.

The crib came with the Laura Ashley bedding from a consignment shop, and that set the palette. "We were going to do the room in bright colors with punches of peony pink and orange until we saw this," Katherine notes.

In the end, they introduced pink by painting the ceiling, trimming the mirror in pink ribbon, adding a pink cover to the changing table, and accessorizing with boxes, small toys, and lampshades.

Two little hats hang on the wall; LiLi loves to wear the one that comes from China. A scroll behind the rocker displays her name in Chinese characters.

When LiLi grows out of her crib, a twin bed will fit nicely in the space, and the toys in the curtain pockets will be replaced with more age-appropriate items. "With no rabbits on the walls, this is the kind of a room that would appeal to someone who doesn't want to be locked into a design motif," says LiLi's mom.

Polymer Modeling Clay, 2 oz.: 5 white, 3 translucent, 3 pearl

Waxed paper

Rolling pin

Rubber alphabet stamps

Pencil

Assorted sea shells

Glass baking dish

Super glue

CRAFTING WITH KIDS

SEASIDE MEMORY PLAQUE

Children love toys and accessories made especially for them. A mom-crafted item in your child's room will provide the personal touch that tells a child she's special while enhancing a decorative theme. In each chapter we include simple craft projects and step-by-step instructions for decorative furnishings to spice up children's rooms. Involve older kids in the craft projects to add to their pride of place and sense of achievement, and for rainy day fun that lasts.

Create this faux marble plaque with polymer clay and alphabet stamps. Add a child's footprint and some pretty shells, and you have a permanent memento of your beach vacation. A quick trick—briefly microwave the clay to soften it and add a footprint. Collect shells, pretty stones, or even small bits of driftwood on your next trip to the beach, and use them to decorate the plaque around the footprint.

INSTRUCTIONS

1. Knead two or three clay blocks of one color together until softened. Repeat for each color until you have kneaded all the clay and softened it. Make long fat logs of each color, and lay them next to each other on waxed paper. Twist the logs together. Fold the twisted piece in half. Roll it into another log and twist it to marbelize the colors. Roll the clay into a tight oval-shaped ball. Make sure that the ball is tight and there are no air bubbles in it. Roll the ball between two sheets of waxed paper with a rolling pin, until you have a plaque about .5" (1 cm) thick and approximately 8.5" (22 cm) long by 6" (15 cm) wide.

2. Place the plaque on a paper towel and microwave on medium for one minute at a time until warm and soft to the touch. Make sure the clay is not hot. Then have a child press a foot into the clay, making an imprint. Use alphabet stamps to imprint the child's name above the footprint. Use a pencil or a bamboo skewer to write the age. Press shells or stones into the clay to mark their position, but remove them before baking the plaque.

3. Bake the plaque in a glass dish following the manufacturer's instructions. Remove the plaque from the oven, and let it cool. Glue the shells and pebbles in their imprints using super glue.

TIPS

• Microwaving polymer clay is tricky. Avoid heating the clay too long or it will crack.

• If you plan to hang your plaque, poke two holes with a pencil at the top of the plaque before baking. Tie on a raffia bow and hang.

MATERIALS

Craft paints: pink, blue, lilac, yellow, white

Wooden Alphabet and Number Blocks

Small container with lid,
5.5" x 4" x 5.5"
(14 cm x 10 cm x 14 cm)

Paintbrush

Patterns: chick, heart, and star

Pencil

Transfer paper

Silver metallic marker
(see instructions on pattern)

Waterbase gloss varnish

Picture, 4.75" x 4.75"
(12 cm x 12 cm)

Straightedge

Craft knife

Decoupage medium

Transparent tape

PAINTED ALPHABET BLOCKS

Decoupaged wooden alphabet and number blocks, complete with sliding lid-top box, are a thoughtful and welcomed gift for a young child. Displayed on a shelf while children are very young, stacking numbers and letters can become part of your decorating theme! Give a fresh new look to this classic learning tool by decorating the blocks to become a three-dimensional puzzle. Simply use pastel acrylic paints, a favorite picture, and decoupage medium. Note: Blocks are suitable for children three years of age and older.

INSTRUCTIONS

1. Prime all of the surfaces that will be painted with a thin coat of white paint. On 16 of the blocks, leave one side unpainted and unvarnished. The puzzle pieces will be applied to the unfinished sides.

2. In the small container, mix peach paint, using 1 part pink to 1 part yellow, and ½ part white. Mix thoroughly. Then, on each of the 32 blocks that will not be a part of the puzzle, paint one side of each block peach. Alternate between painting the solid sides and the letter or number sides of the blocks. Paint just the raised portion-the letter or number itself and the border. Paint white onto the background area of the letters and numbers. Let each color dry completely before painting the next color. Continue painting one side of each block with a new color until all blocks are completed—with the exception of the one unpainted side of the 16 blocks that will be used for the puzzle.

3. Place a sheet of transfer paper underneath the chick pattern. Trace the drawing with the pencil onto the carbon paper. Place the transfer paper face down on the lid and rub the back with a pencil. Paint the lid and let dry. Transfer the heart pattern to the side of the box using transfer paper. Paint the side of the box, let dry, then repeat on other side of box and allow to dry. Following the same process, transfer the star pattern onto the front of the box. Paint and let dry. Repeat on the back of the box and allow to dry.

4. Apply one coat of varnish to all of the painted surfaces. Tape the picture to a cutting surface. Using a straightedge, measure and mark the picture into sixteen 1³⁄₁₆" x 1³⁄₁₆" (3.15 cm x 3.15 cm) squares. Use the straightedge and a craft knife to cut the picture along the markings.

5. Use the paintbrush to apply decoupage medium to the back of one picture piece. Adhere to the unfinished side of the block. Repeat until all of the pieces have been affixed to each of the 16 blocks. Let dry. Apply a final coat of varnish over the picture pieces. Allow everything to dry for 24 hours before putting the blocks back into the box.

TIPS

• When painting with yellow, paint only the solid sides of the blocks, not the letter or number sides. Yellow does not show up well on a white background.

• Be sure to work on a clean surface, as the paint can get scuffed or dirty before the varnish is applied.

• Find an interesting picture for the puzzle face—draw a picture, cut out a magazine or book page, or make a color copy of a favorite book illustration or photo to size. Do not use an actual photograph or any prints on heavy paper.

The ABCs of Decorating
Painted Wooden Letters

WITH THESE DECORATIVE WOODEN ALPHABET LETTERS, *it's as easy as ABC to create a charming nursery accent. Choose colors to coordinate with the room's decor or personalize the project further by spelling out the baby's name. Even a beginner can easily create the heart/leaf patterns shown here using a specially formulated "enamel" craft paint. The finished letters can be displayed on a shelf or dresser top or be adhered to the wall or a door.*

Materials:

5" (13 cm) wooden letters

Décor-it! enamel-like paints: sea blue, lemon, apricot, kelly green, grass green, magenta

1" foam brushes

Fine-grade sanding sponge

Tack cloth

Stylus

Instructions

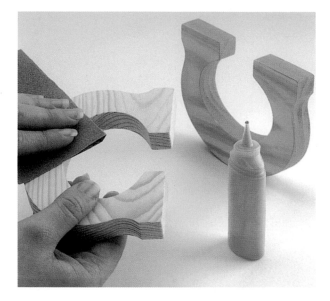

1. Sand each wooden letter with a fine-grade sanding sponge, and wipe clean with a tack cloth. Using a foam brush, paint the edges and back of each letter. Let dry, and then paint a second coat. Let dry overnight.

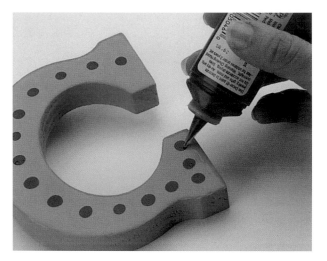

2. Choose two coordinating colors of Décor-it! paint. Using the applicator tip, flow the first color generously to the unpainted front surface of the wooden letter, making sure the coverage extends to the edges. While the first color is still very wet, apply dots of the second color along the center of the letter, spacing them about a dot's width apart.

A Word About

What Baby Sees

Adults tend to think of babies in terms of soft pastels, but the fact is that newborns, in particular, are most drawn to bold shapes in black, white, and red. If you really want to attract their attention, create some accents with strong contrasts in color and value. As the baby becomes more aware of her surroundings beyond the crib, she will appreciate the rich environment you provide.

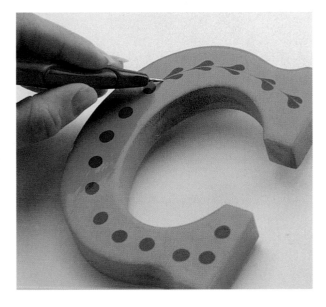

3. Beginning just beyond the edge of the first dot, drag the pointed edge of the stylus through the center of the dots. The special formulation of the paint will cause the colors to swirl, creating a leaf or heart design. Let dry completely. Use the same technique with different colors until you have decorated all of the letters.

Variation

Personalize any baby's room by using bright, bold primary colors to spell out the baby's name. Then use Décor-it! paint to embellish the letters with the design of your choice. The palette shown includes red, yellow, blue, white, and magenta. Have fun and be creative!

Modern

ABC Lamp Shades

This project is everything modern: bold colors, clean lettering, stylish lines. The strong shadow is broken away from the main letter, creating an empty moat of background color between shadow and letter. Painted lamp shades create subtle lighting effects in your home, shading and directing the light more completely than unpainted shades. The strong colors used here are perfect for a child's room, and you can add other accents in a similar style: paint an ABC border on the walls, paint letters on dresser drawers, or initials on a coat rack.

For this project you will need:

- purchased lamp shades
- Alphabet lettering guide
- tracing paper
- white transfer paper
- pen
- acrylic paint in bright red, yellow-orange, dark violet, and white
- foam brushes
- small flat brush
- small round brush
- very small round brush or spotting brush

Lettering Technique

A border inserted between a letter and its shadow creates a stylish graphic element and another opportunity to add color to a design.

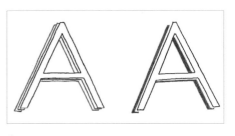

1.

1. Enlarge the alphabet guide letters to a size big enough to fill one face of a lamp shade. Check the size with the widest letter that you'll transfer. Outline the letter on tracing paper three times as shown, shifting the letter down and to the left each time (left). The outlines that create the final effect are the first letter and the final letter minus the area covered by the middle letter (right).

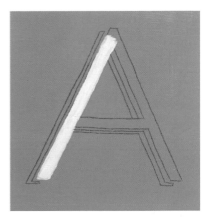

2.

2. Transfer the final outlines to a lamp shade already base-coated with acrylic paint. White transfer paper is recommended because it's less messy than blue or graphite (though graphite paper is shown here for greater contrast). Center the letter carefully on the lamp shade face—each letter should sit on the same baseline for consistency, and the main (white) letter should be centered from side to side. Begin filling in the main letter with white acrylic paint and a small flat brush. *Tip:* Check the coverage of the base coat of paint by turning the lamp on with the shade in place. You'll immediately see areas that need more paint.

3.

3. Continue painting the main letter with white paint, using a very small round or spotting brush to fill in detail in tight corners. You'll probably need to paint at least two or three coats of white for solid coverage over a darker color. Let dry. Paint the shadows with the base color used on another lamp shade panel and the small round brush. It's easy to correct mistakes with very small liner brush and the base color paint. When finished and completely dry, wipe with a damp soft cloth to remove transfer residue.

ABCD **Variation** The bright, playful colors shown here may not work with every decor! Try a subtle and sophisticated palette of moss green with gray-blue shadows in all lowercase letters for a more subdued accent piece.

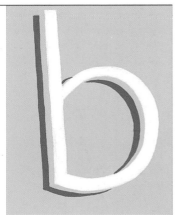

"Eat Your Peas" Decoupage Bowls

Hand-drawn letters, cut out of vibrant decorative paper and decoupaged onto wooden bowls, offer a commanding yet playful voice in your kitchen. These humorous decorative bowls are perfect to hang in a row over a kitchen window, by the dinner table, or even in a child's room. The bright painted background was created with animators' vinyl paint, a bright, highly pigmented paint used to color cartoon cels. Decoupaged letters work well with many crafts—try jewelry boxes, serving trays, frames, even furniture.

For this project you will need:

3 small wooden bowls

animators' vinyl paint (or acrylic paint) in your desired colors

round and flat paintbrushes

tracing paper

pencil

transfer paper

artists' colored paper in two shades (origami paper or graphic artists' color swatch paper works well)

craft knife

white craft glue

decoupage medium

foam brush

fine sandpaper

Lettering Technique

Playful hand-drawn letters become bright and dimensional when cut from colored paper and decoupaged on a wooden surface.

1.

1. Sketch your desired letters on tracing paper. We used simple lower-case forms so they would have nice, clean lines. Notice how the strokes of the e and the a don't close the letterform—this looks contemporary and playful, and adds a dynamic variation when pasted on top of the more solid backing letter. Don't worry about lining the letters evenly on a baseline; they'll look more interesting if they're jumbled a bit, and you'll be cutting them out separately, anyway.

2.

2. When you have the letters drawn to your satisfaction, sketch an outline around the whole letter. Try to keep a regular space between the inside and outside letterforms, and fill in the closing strokes of the letters, if desired. With transfer paper and a pen, transfer the inside lines to the light shade of artists' colored paper, and transfer the outside lines to a darker shade of artists' colored paper. Cut out the letters from the colored paper with a craft knife. There's no need to cut perfectly straight lines—variations in stroke thickness add to the handmade look of the final piece.

3.

3. Glue the letters onto prepainted wooden bowls with white craft glue. Paste the larger, darker letters first, then paste the smaller, lighter letters on top. Place the letters in a dynamic arrangement, with some letters leaning left and others leaning right for variation. Let dry completely. Apply four to five coats of decoupage medium to each bowl according to manufacturer's directions, letting dry and lightly sanding between coats with fine sandpaper for a smooth finish.

Variation The strong solid colors used in the project are a perfect complement to the decorative painting in the bowls, but for a project using letters only, try decorating the inside letters with permanent markers or paint before decoupaging them to the craft surface. Test your chosen colors with decoupage medium before using it on the final project to be sure they are color fast.

ROOM TO GROW

CHILDREN'S BEDROOMS

When you decorate your children's rooms, you are doing more than making beautiful, colorful, and pleasant spaces—you are creating places of comfort and security. This environment, created with the colors, fabrics, wallpapers, and accessories you choose, may make a significant contribution to your children's sense of self and overall development—so make sure you have a room that pleases them, that they feel is a private haven.

Decorating and furnishing your children's rooms also can nourish their imaginations, teach important lessons, and encourage dialog. As you consider design options, include your children in the discussion. Give them a vote, which will help later with ownership and responsibility lessons. Of course, the further your children's communication skills advance, the more their individualism will surface. You will see their tastes emerge as they toss objects and ideas aside or express a preference for specific colors, patterns—even decorative objects. While preference phases are likely to come and go, it is important for parents to hear about them and discuss them with their children.

Use this chapter to find out how to decorate around the tricky transition from crib to bed, how to choose the style of furnishing that's right for you and your children, and how to decorate with pattern and color to create a flexible but fun design for your children's bedrooms. Then, share this information with them and ask questions about what they see and think. This will give you a chance to point out what you think is important for them to have in their room.

Left: A stuffed treasure and a beloved story are all within easy reach when bedtime rolls around.

Piece by Piece

When the great moment of moving your toddler from crib to bed comes, this one-time sanctuary of sleep and lullabies becomes your child's safe haven and a comfortable and cozy place for him to keep his treasures. Start your decorating scheme by considering the most costly and largest pieces in your child's room: the furniture—a bed, bureau, bedside table, bookcase or shelving, and side chairs.

The good news is today's choices are myriad: You can find beds that are small versions of antique sleigh and brass beds, and beds in clean country, ultrasleek contemporary, and fantasy shapes. Choose natural wood tones or white frames for the greatest design flexibility. Consider getting your child a bed in the Shaker style; its simple, classic lines are always in fashion and blend well with other furniture styles. For a more modern look, select fabric-covered, padded headboards that can hook onto an existing twin bed frame. Slip off the covers for easy cleaning, or replace with neutral or white fabric to create a different look in your child's bedroom.

With the bed in neutral colors, let fabrics, wall coverings, and rugs take the lead. Cover the bed with colorful patterns of animals, houses, stars, clouds, or moons. Cover cool floors with area rugs that pick up the theme. Unite disparate patterns with bed skirts, quilts, or comforters in solid hues.

Adaptability is key, so explore convertible designs—beds that grow and change as your child does. Consider choosing a crib that can convert to a toddler's bed, then a twin, and later a double. This is also a good option because you can choose good construction over a trendy color, shape, or style, and make one purchase that will last many years.

Above: Keep floors and beds natural or white to let the focus remain on the pretty patterns and one or two pieces of painted furniture. To create a delightful, engaging room, take a visual theme from a wallpaper border, such as this dressing-up vignette, and let drapes echo the theme. Choose a complementary yet simple, repetitive pattern for the rest of the wall. And don't forget a place for your children's life trophies, such as this fabric-covered bulletin board.

Above: Built-in bunk beds turn a confined space, such as the dormer side of a room, into cozy sleeping quarters for kids. You can build in a multitude of storage options: bookshelves, drawers beneath the lower bunk, and closet space. Decorate bunk bed openings with ornamental shapes to make the space even more magical for your children.

Or, to navigate that tricky transition from crib to twin bed, use a small trundle bed that slides under a larger twin bed, to which the child can graduate eventually. The trundle will come in handy later for a slumber party guest.

Of course, safety is the first consideration when a toddler moves from a crib to a regular bed, whether a twin, double, or bunk bed. Install removable safety bars on both sides of the bed, no matter what the style. Do not allow children under the age of six to sleep on a top bunk, even with bars. For the sake of safety, make sure the spaces between the guard rails and the mattress or bars at the end of the bed are narrower than 3.5 inches (9 cm).

If your children share a room, consider getting bunk beds. Children love the coziness created by the overhead bed and the adventure of using a ladder. In general, bunk beds are fun (they make a great backbone for a massive tent), and they save on floor space. Should a conflict arise over who gets to sleep on top, transform the disagreement into an opportunity to learn to share—have them take turns.

When choosing a chest of drawers, take into account your habits and those of your child, which count in the management of your child's room. Be realistic—for example, don't buy that extra piece of furniture with six drawers if you prefer (or if it's quicker for you) to put clean clothes on shelves.

Think, too, about what will be easier and more manageable for your children to deal with when you delegate to them the responsibility of folding or storing clothes. A small bureau may work well in combination with open shelves and wall pegs for hanging things like shirts and pants. The advantage of shelves and pegs is that they can be installed at your children's height for easy access.

Set aside a place for their books, toys, stuffed animals, and special little treasures. It's important for children to know where their things are; it sets and holds the rhythm of familiarity and repetition—the qualities that give them comfort and security.

Create a wish list of the major pieces of furniture, then plan the layout of the furniture in the room, being sensitive to its relationship with the rest of the house. If you live in a condominium or apartment, place the bed on an inside wall, away from a noisy hallway. In a single-family home, consider siting the bed with a good view of a window so you can improvise a bedtime story while your child is stargazing or listening to the crickets and crows. Don't forget to take precautions, such as keeping the bed away from wall heaters and dangling shade strings. Likewise, plan for convenience; set the bed near outlets so you can install a night-light and reading light.

Finally, before you make any major furniture purchase, ask yourself these two questions:

1. **Do you plan to stay in this home for the next five years?** If not, consider these short-term, cost-effective decorating ideas: Paint your walls instead of papering; hang a swag valence over windows instead of draperies; adorn the walls with lots of family photos that go with you wherever you move; paint the floors and use area rugs instead of buying wall-to-wall carpet.

Above: Give your child a good view of a window, where they can stargaze, listen to crickets and birds, or daydream. A padded headboard provides a soft indigo backdrop that complements the whimsical wall border and bed linens.

Below: Let stuffed animals and toys reside in a special place, such as atop an unused fireplace mantel or bookshelf. If you are short on wall space, hang a shelf, rack, or ledge above the nightstand or bureau.

2. **Will this room be shared with a sibling?** For example, if you have a two-year-old and a ten-month-old, are you going to put them together in one bedroom? If so, here are some ideas for navigating sibling seas: If your kids are close in age, buy furniture that can be used by both to save money and floor space; purchase an armoire and give half to each for clothing storage; color-code wooden clothes pegs on the wall for hanging up clothes; buy one bookcase and organize the books so it's split for each. As the ten-month-old catches up with the two-year-old in tastes and needs, this system can also teach them about sharing.

Room for Creativity

An ideal technique for boosting your children's sense of comfort and pleasure is to get them involved in the design of their own room. There are no rules on how to do this, and each child's ability to communicate likes and dislikes is highly individual.

Children develop their taste buds, if you will, as early as two. For a little girl who loves ballet classes or horseback riding, choosing wallpaper with those kinds of images pleases her, feeds her imagination, keeps the interest alive, and even relaxes her when she's daydreaming in her bed. Likewise, for a little boy, seeing the things he is most interested in on his walls or floor, or on the drapery, does the same. As you're probably already attuned to your child's interests, look for ways to decorate his or her room judiciously. Keep the decorating reference to their interests meaningful by adding to decor carefully. Install wallpaper borders or artwork at the child's height, at baseboards, or at windowsill level.

Left: Your children's bedroom is as individual as they are. If adventure and travel are what they love, be playful with color and accessories.

Above: Decorate with wallpaper borders that tell a story—the cow jumping over the moon will come in handy to illustrate goodnight stories. Make sure you position the border at kid height, at the top of the chair rail or above the baseboard.

Look to colorful wallpapers, rugs, curtains, and lamps that express your children's interests, whether they are boats, trucks, or animals. These images also help you and your children talk and provide cues for little life lessons you may want to instill. You can point to the cow, or moon, or boat, and begin a spelling lesson, or make up a story with your child.

Decorating options that accomplish this include blackboard paint (which allows you to devote part of a wall to freedom of expression or a spelling lesson) and stick-on glow-in-the-dark stars. Another option is washable wallpaper that comes with loose fish or butterflies that your children can place anywhere on the wall.

Depending on how flexible you are, you can create a room that gives you freedom to change themes frequently without spending a fortune. One way you can do this is to divide the room into decorating areas. For example, you can paint or use simple patterned wallpaper on the lower levels of the walls and put the theme on the borders. You can also cover an entire wall (the lower half) with blackboard paint and introduce the border and wallpaper where it stops.

Above: Multicolored butterflies float across the wallpaper, curtains, and bedcovers to make this treetop-level room a magical place. Maintain the light, playful feeling with a painted wood floor—an easy decorating project for any mom or dad.

girls' bedrooms

Coordinating chintz fabrics? Floor-to-ceiling toile? Decoration in your daughter's bedroom doesn't have to be limited to arch-feminine choices. Whether dainty or tomboyish, every girl has an opinion on her surroundings and it won't necessarily mesh with yours. Take the time to listen to your daughter's desires before outfitting her room in all pink. Let her make choices regarding color and bedding. Maybe graphic stripes or a windowpane check suit her better, with feminine touches in smaller doses. Or maybe she feels more at ease with soft-green or blue-painted walls instead of classic pink. If her choices are traditional, that's fine, too. She should feel comfortable in her own space. Encourage her to develop her own style, but try to stay away from ultra-trendy choices that she'll outgrow practically overnight.

Although the wisest big-furniture purchases are the ones that work long term, you can have fun with smaller pieces, like bedside tables or benches. They don't have to match; just make sure that they're the right height for the child's bed and that they have enough surface area for a reading lamp, clock, and books for nighttime stories.

Combine the Bedroom and Playroom

If the bedroom will double as a play area, reserve space on the bookshelves or in a corner of the room for doll furniture, stuffed animals, or even a small, child-size table and chairs for playtime. These can easily be replaced with a desk and chair as your daughter enters school and outgrows them. Bins for toys and other objects are a good way to organize, and can be stacked in a closet or a quiet corner. A colorful trunk can serve both as a storage unit and a low bench. Paint it a fun color, and top it off with a removable cushion to make it fit into the room's color scheme.

Hang framed museum prints or other artwork on the walls, or prop them up on bracketed shelves. You can even make an educational trip to a local museum to let your daughter pick out her favorite artwork. Prints are an inexpensive way to decorate, adding tons of style that can please you both and can help promote an appreciation of art at the same time. An oversize bulletin board with a frame-style border is another way to provide space for her to pin up magazine clippings along with her favorite photographs and memorabilia.

OPPOSITE Lavender gets an ultracool update in this girl's bedroom. Choose a classic-white bed frame and nightstand for furniture that will still look great with any color scheme if the occupant decides she isn't into lavender anymore and wants to redecorate. The bank of pillows makes the bed a comfortable lounging spot.

LEFT A daybed like this iron campaign-style version can moonlight as a child's trundle bed. Paint the walls a color like this peachy pink for an instant dose of femininity, and let your daughter choose her own bedding.

KID-FRIENDLY: wall treatments

PAINT

When it comes time to paint or cover walls in a child's room, so many options are available that it can make your head spin. Paints are offered in various finishes, from flat, the most matte looking, to shiny, high-gloss latex paints with eggshell finishes in between. How do you know what's best for your children? Although they're all safe, paint with the most latex is usually reserved for surfaces other than drywall, because it has a flashier, shinier look. So you might consider sticking to a flat or eggshell finish or to a less-concentrated mix of latex. Make sure the paint you choose is easy to clean, too. Keep in mind that flat paint doesn't clean well. Although it may be preferable aesthetically, smudges and dirty handprints mar matte paint very quickly. The less absorbent the paint, the easier it is to erase dirty handprints, magic markers, and other common mishaps.

Be Careful of Lead Paint

If you're renovating an old house, however, other safety precautions must be observed. Find out whether there is old lead paint already on the walls, possibly under many coats of newer paint. If so, avoid stripping or sanding the walls yourself. Call in qualified deleading experts, and make sure the children stay out of the house until the work is done. Paint dust is a common source of lead poisoning in small children.

BORDERS—WALLPAPERED OR HAND-PAINTED

Wallpaper borders and hand-painted details can add a whimsical or pretty touch in a child's bedroom. Chintz flower borders can be lovely in a girl's room. Or, if you want to indulge in cartoon characters or car motifs in primary colors, a border is delightfully welcome in a nursery or young child's room, and is less overpowering than wallpapering the entire room (as well as easier to re-do when the child has outgrown the style). Keep in mind that when a scratch or an errant crayon marks up a papered wall, there's hardly ever a remedy, whereas painted walls can be repainted or patched up with a touch of extra paint. Hand-painted friezes near the ceiling are out of reach and thus less likely to be sullied when children are at play. Use a stencil if you're doing it yourself, or create your own design that features your child's favorite motif.

Durable, simple, and easy-to-clean should be the mantra for kid-friendly walls. The less fussy your child's walls are, the easier they'll be to maintain.

OPPOSITE Matching fabrics all over the room can be kid-friendly and cohesive, as in the animal-print coverlet, roman shades, and wallpaper border that run riot in this bedroom. Tame prints by using neutral patterns in a different scale and lots of white or neutral colors alongside them.

SURFACE SIMPLICITY

· Pick a paint finish that's easy to clean.

· Test for lead before stripping old paint from walls.

· Add a wallpaper border or hand-painted details for a fun touch.

· Keep some paint close at hand in case touch-ups are needed.

· Stick to simple surfaces for practicality.

boys' bedrooms

The same rules apply in a boy's room. Make an effort to include your son in your decorating decisions, because he may need more coercion. Begin with simple questions, like what his favorite color is. It may range from a nautical blue to a hunter green to a neutral tan, but being asked will make him feel involved. Decorate the room with reminders of his personal pastimes or hobbies. If he's a sports fan, he'll probably delight in sports photographs or drawings hanging on the wall or a framed autograph from a favorite team or game. If he's a budding fishermen, he might enjoy nautical artifacts or maps. Likewise, if he's interested in chess, dinosaurs, or architecture, his room should reflect those interests, not only to enhance the room's personality but also to encourage your child's passions.

Design a Space That Grows with Your Child

Invest in sturdy furniture for growing boys. There may be lots of wear and tear involved for active kids. Bunk beds are always a great option, and they save space. Constructing perpendicular bunks creates a loft area underneath for a desk and bookshelves, too, providing room for a sleepover as well as a cozy space to study. A desk for homework in any child's room is a must. Simply make sure it can accommodate a growing child's height. The accompanying chair should also have adjustable seat and back height. For the play area of a bedroom, plenty of storage space is needed. Whether games and toys are stowed away in a trunk or in boxes stacked in the closet and under the bed, encourage organization whenever possible. If every toy has a prescribed space in the bookshelf, closet, or trunk, picking up becomes much simpler.

Let boys have a hand in do-it-yourself decorating, too. If they want to pass on tie-dyed sheets, let them come up with other ideas. Maybe they'll want to display a collection of model planes, ticket stubs, or hats gathered from vacation spots. Give your child an art wall where his imagination can run wild and he can decorate however he likes, even with artwork done at school.

OPPOSITE Don't consider only dark shades for a boy's room; paint walls a cheery taxicab yellow. Throw in accents like this sports-motif carpet and matching bedding. A loft area doubles the available play space.

shared bedrooms

Cramped space doesn't have to mean scrimping on style. When there aren't enough bedrooms to go around and your children need to double up, an extra dose of attention is needed. Personalizing is extra-important for them to mark their own territory. Create separate havens within the same room by designating at least some part of the room as each child's own space.

Two halves don't necessarily make a whole, though. Avoid a disparate look by giving kids options within a limited range of color and furniture choices. A blue-and-green plaid comforter can coordinate with a solid matching hue on another bed. For a laid-back attitude, mismatched furniture from the same manufacturer fits equally well without the stuffiness of a bedroom set, as long as styles don't clash. Use one similar element—like color, shape, or style—to tie it all together. Or if you'd prefer to have matching bedspreads and furniture, maybe the kids can cast their vote on their bedside table, a lamp, or the artwork above the headboard.

Divide the Space Equally

Space-savvy furniture, like bunk beds or a desk unit that accommodates two, is a valuable asset in a shared bedroom. Lay out the room as symmetrically as possible to avoid quarrels over space with a division in the middle. Back-to-back desks, bookcases, or a small table can mark territory. Designate separate storage areas, like armoires or chests, or divide drawers and closet space evenly in a central storage space. A canopied bed or a mosquito net made out of a lightweight fabric hung from above also creates the illusion of privacy within a shared bedroom. When a child craves alone time, the fabric can be pulled down along the sides.

If a shared bedroom is in a vacation home or weekend house, rules and divisions can be more relaxed. The shorter amount of time spent there reduces potential problems in room sharing. Armoires can be shared and beds interchangeable, although decorative details that give a room its style are just as important.

OPPOSITE Twin beds get a separate-but-equal treatment in this shared bedroom. Although they share a galvanized metal bedside table, it has separate drawers, and the wainscoted ledge allows each inhabitant to personalize her own side by displaying art.

ABOVE Sleek, modern built-in bunks make great use of space. Use plenty of soft pillows to ensure comfort when lounging or reading in bed as well as when sleeping. These beach house bunks don't need be personalized because their occupants don't live here full-time, but with pure-white bedding and bright pillows, they're highly inviting.

SHOPPING: beds

BUY STURDY AND SAFE

When you're in the market for that restful place for your kids to lay their heads, versatile and classic beds are ideal. For cribs that transform into junior beds, check out the website www.PoshTots.com for a stylish, kid-size sleigh crib or bed. Bunk beds and trundles can be found virtually anywhere. If you're buying a first junior-size bed, make sure that it isn't too high above the ground and that its sides are high enough to prevent rolling out of bed. You can never be too cautious when it comes to safety, even in the bedroom. If you choose to skip the junior bed and go straight to a twin, temporary railings that prevent roll-outs are sold everywhere kids' furniture is sold. For older children, if bunk beds fit the bill, make sure that ladders and slats are sturdy enough and that the top bunk bed has side rails. Trundle beds are usually outfitted with heavy hardware. Before buying one, make sure that the frame is strong enough to hold a mattress (and to withstand a little bouncing) and that the trundle is easy enough for a child to pull out. Look for other options on trundles, too, like the ability to replace the trundle with storage drawers.

Invest in sturdy and well-designed frames or headboards that will last throughout the years. Children can be active sleepers. Make sure there are no sharp edges or hard surfaces that kids can unknowingly hurt themselves on in the middle of the night. Wood or metal beds are long-lasting choices when made well. If you decide on an iron frame, stock your child's bed with plenty of pillows to prevent his or her head from bumping against the hard metal. For a fantastical child's room, beds shaped like cars, rockets, or boats are a fun option, although these will be outgrown in a few years. Canopy beds, which require high ceilings and a bit more space, are also wonderfully private, especially in a shared bedroom. You can create your own canopy by draping fabric from hooks or a cornice attached to the ceiling. A twin bed in a corner can be curtained off for a similar effect. Another option, if you don't want to invest in an entire bed frame, is to use an upholstered headboard—for example, a simple, rectangular shape covered in fabric like simple duck canvas or more elaborate baroque silhouettes tufted with the fabric of your choice. Headboard slipcovers are particularly versatile, and having a few ready-made ones on hand can provide easy, mood-altering switches.

SELECT THE BEST MATTRESS

A good mattress is just as important as a safe and well-made bed. Always buy the best mattress that you can afford. Bring your children along with you to test out the comfort level. Once you buy one, make sure to rotate it periodically to keep the springs functioning well and flip it from time to time, too.

ABOVE A bed with high sides like this wooden one is an ideal choice for a first bed. The sides prevent a toddler from rolling out, and a high headboard and footboard enclose the bed, making its occupant feel safe and secure.

SWEET DREAMS

- If you're looking for practicality, consider a convertible bed that goes from crib to twin, or a bunk bed that becomes a trundle.

- Test drive beds with any mechanisms like ladders or drawers.

- Always invest in a well-made bed if you're looking for longevity. Sturdy wood or metal are two materials that typically last.

- Avoid sharp corners in a child's bed.

- Use a canopy bed to give your child a little extra privacy.

- Headboards with removable slipcovers are a less-costly alternative to buying a full bed frame, but they're equally stylish.

- Buy the best-quality mattress you can afford.

DESIGNING **FAMILY SPACES**

Today, design themes for our homes are more relaxed than ever before; the focus is now on comfort, practicality, and at-home pleasures. This approach has caught on in the city as well as the suburbs, and it bodes well for those raising families. With designers and architects attuned to this trend, we have more choices to help us create homes that embrace family life.

Children should be welcome everywhere in the house:

You can choose fabrics, fabric protectors, floor coverings, paints, and layouts that can make your home attractive and child-friendly.

Here are ways to design the public rooms in your home with children in mind.

Entryways

With children and pets filing through this space all day long, the entry is often a difficult place to keep tidy. If you do not have the luxury of a mud room or a back door, shoes, schoolbooks, mail, and sports equipment can all end up here for a portion of the day.

Lots of little hands and muddy feet can keep you in a perpetual state of cleaning.

Above: These rounded granite countertop corners are perfect for a home with children, as are the bookshelves. Notice, too, that the kitchen chairs are covered in fabric. This gives a dressier look to the room, and if you get a washable fabric, you don't have to be concerned about spills or stains.

Above: This pup opted for sitting on the tile floor instead of the washable rag rug, but that's okay because you can vacuum his hair off the tile in a flash. When he brings in mud on his feet, a damp sponge mop will pick it right up.

Here are tips on how to make this space easy to live with:

- Choose a floor that can be washed with soap and water. Tile, stone, and linoleum can all work.
- Paint the walls and doors in the entry with a semigloss paint so you can quickly clean smudges. Keep paper towels and glass cleaner in a nearby cupboard or closet. It's a good idea to keep a mop or broom nearby too.
- Provide attractive storage options. If your children come in and take off their shoes, give them a place to put them other than the floor. Use an old trunk or a bench with storage under the seat as a shoe bin. Have another for balls and bats. Keep your mail and theirs, in separate open wooden boxes on a shelf or table, or find some interesting baskets that can become part of the design landscape. For keys that are invariably tossed here and

Above: Here is a breakfast nook that is child-friendly and easy to keep clean. The wooden tabletop—if treated with natural wax—will repel spills. The light wood chairs are easy to move and won't scratch the tile floor if they're dragged about.

Bottom Right: Who wouldn't love to have breakfast in this cheery room? The painted wood chairs and table can all be cleaned easily, and the colorful rug below catches crumbs. Don't worry about spilling on a waxed wood floor; liquid just beads, and you can pick it up with a paper towel.

there, consider a key rack or a specific basket or little box. Install a nice row of pegs to hold coats and jackets that might otherwise end up thrown over chairs. Don't forget to install pegs at your children's height!

- If the dog habitually waits for you by the front door and leaves a pile of hair and a wet bone, solve the problem by putting an extra dog bed or a dark-colored rug there. Neither the slurp nor the hair will show up. Choose a washable cover for the bed and, if you like, a washable rug.

Kitchens

More and more kitchens these days are open rooms that give whoever is cooking dinner the ability to chat with family members in other areas of the house.

If you are in the planning stage of a kitchen layout, consider creating one big, open room. Also, think about installing countertop surfaces and cupboard knobs that can be easily cleaned with a wet sponge. Look for soft,

rounded edges on counters rather than hard, square ones that could hurt when a child rounds a corner too fast and goes bump!

Another popular design element is bookshelves for storing cookbooks. Should you have them or build them, put some children's books or magazines on the lower shelves so children can browse and chat with you while you chop or knead.

If you have a growing family, with some children old enough to help in the kitchen, consider arranging storage areas so they can have access to unbreakable dishes and glasses and the family's napkins, wooden salad bowl, and tongs.

For flooring, choose a surface that's easy to clean and a pattern that won't show every speck of dirt. Stone, tile, marble, synthetic tile, and wood can all be swept clean with a damp mop. Of course, if you have very small children who will undoubtedly spill on this surface, think about how it will behave when wet. Will it turn into a slip-and-slide floor?

If you plan to put a rug in front of the sink or in the doorway, choose one with a no-skid back or put a rubber pad under it.

Consider purchasing wooden chairs instead of metal; they are less apt to hurt if a child bumps into them, they are easier to handle, and if the chair topples over or is dragged, it won't scratch the floor.

If you prefer a more sophisticated look, you can cover chairs with fabric. Choose a washable fabric that's got Velcro to keep it snug (no zippers to hurt), and treat it with a stain-resistant spray.

Of course, if you have toddlers, you must childproof the kitchen by moving all cleaning fluids and dangerous items into high cupboards. Try to put things that will interest the toddlers in the lower cupboards—pots and pans and wooden spoons; for less noise, fill low cupboards with play kitchen toys.

Above: This room has lots of childproof elements—a no-fuss wooden coffee table, a sisal rug (easy to clean; let spilled food dry, then vacuum), bookshelves the whole family can share, and washable slipcovers all around. Everyone can enjoy this pretty room.

Dens, Living Rooms, and Porches

In these busy rooms, choose furnishings, colors, and fabrics wisely. In heavy-traffic areas, choose rugs with complex patterns and deep, rich colors so the dirt won't show. Do the same for the main rugs too, especially if you have toddlers. Again, consider washable semigloss paint, washable wallpaper, or wallpaper above the touch line.

Don't worry if white is your favorite color for your couches. Just use slipcovers that are washable and tuck paper towels into the sides of every seat so you can catch a spill when it happens. If you prefer to take your chances with fancier fabrics that require professional cleaning, treat them with stain inhibitors.

With toddlers, think twice about your coffee table. Glass should not be your first choice. It may be pretty, but many a child has gotten a black eye from a glass corner. While you can put a protective cover on it, that defeats the purpose of the table's look! So choose wood or some other material without sharp corners. Also, it's a good idea to have a drawer or two in the table for storing books or games.

Of course, the more bookshelves you have in these rooms, the better. You can store reading materials, games, and dry art supplies on them. What better way to encourage reading and family time?

In less formal rooms, like porches and sunrooms, consider furniture that's light to move about and that's bright, cheery, and welcoming. Dovetail adult items and children's, so your children really feel integrated throughout your home.

PATTERNS, COLORS, AND **TIMELESS THEMES**

Children want color, character, and life in their bedroom, so look for fabrics and wallpaper that offer style and sophistication without depending on the latest cartoon fad. Select furnishings with a white or natural finish, which makes a neutral backdrop for decorating. Paint trim and walls with light pastels, white, or neutral colors.

Choose themes that relate to your child's **activities and dreams** —boats, bicycles, ballet, horses, stars, flowers, circus animals, kings, and queens.

When you design around a theme, introduce **one large element** keyed to that theme rather than a host of small ones. Build a circus theme by hanging a clown mobile and covering the bed with linens that match. Create a flower theme by laying flower-shaped throw rugs, then hanging curtains keyed to their color scheme.

Remember that **adaptability** is vital when selecting your child's bedroom fashions. Pick linens and accessories that can be adapted as the child grows from toddler to elementary school student to teenager. Mix classic motifs such as toile, animals, or even chintz with stripes, gingham, or checkerboard patterns to allow a more sophisticated look later on.

Reinforce a theme with **accessories.** For example, if your son loves the circus, help him collect small circus toys or stuffed animals that can be displayed on a shelf or chair top.

Create a **neutral or white backdrop** for the patterns, fabrics, and collections in your child's room. Paint the trim white and select white curtains. Look for pastel bed linens and cloth.

For little girls, anticipate the transition from a sweet, girlish style to a powerful, modern teenage scheme. Select **soft pastels** and **storybook drawings** that will give you the freedom to punch up color and accent themes with rugs, wall art, or deeper hues of complementary colors via painted furniture.

DECORATING TO BUILD **SELF-ESTEEM**

Once you've made your child's room comfortable and inviting, think about ways to nourish their sense of self and to build their confidence through decor. For example, experts who study children know that as soon as they understand the concept of growing up, they begin to strive to achieve that. Make marking time and growth a design element in their rooms.

Devote a portion of a child's bedroom or playroom wall to **measuring height.** Paint or glue a yardstick on the wall and decorate it with your child's photos and special occasions that mark time.

Buy an inexpensive **bulletin board** and make a family project out of painting and decorating it. Use it as a display area for showing off school drawings, report cards, and homework with high marks.

Reserve a portion of a wall for rotating **photos that capture those special moments** you're always recording: baseball practice, taking the training wheels off a bicycle, or a first skating lesson.

Maintain a **row of photos** of each child—from birth onward—so they can see how they've grown and changed.

Start a **birthday party bulletin board** where photos and special cards hang.

If Jack's parents were planning to redesign his room, they could use this drawing to prompt a discussion on the subject. Meanwhile, here are tips for adding a bit mor fun to a child's room:

- 🐦 The elevator is certainly not realistic, nor is the swing set, but maybe a faux painting on the wall behind the bed could enliven the room. It could picture a swing set or even an elevator.

- 🐕 The bunk bed access could be made more amusing by painting or decorating the ladder.

- 🚢 Another area to explore for decorating came from Boston designer Eva Dewitz, who likes to decorate television sets. Jack could work with his parents to decorate a television or the family computer. Some things that could be glued on for fun are building blocks, rods and spools, dominos, marbles, or action toys.

DECORATING TIPS
FROM THE KIDS

Jack

Jack, eight and a half years old, explained to me that this picture is of his bunk bed, and the blue object is an elevator he wished he had next to the bed. He also drew a swing set next to the bunk bed. Jack included his stuffed animals on his bed surface, added his blanket and pillow, and drew in his windows to show how his bed sits in the room.

Jack

Leah

When Leah was asked what she wished she had in her room, she drew two things: a girl in a cozy chair and her sister, Anna, in bed. She really loves sharing a room with her sister. To four-year-olds, being cuddly and secure takes the lead over design!

To make a child's room more cuddly, parents could consider these options:

- Adding a down comforter to the bed and covering it with fabric that depicts cuddly things—animals, kittens, puppies, bunnies.

- Warming up the light in her room by choosing low-watt bulbs and choosing lamps with bases that depict storybook characters.

- Exploring the cozy chair idea. Does Leah want a chair for herself or one where she would sit on mom's or dad's lap for a story? Both are achievable, affordable, and could make bedtime a more pleasant experience. Perhaps a beanbag chair with a big, fluffy throw would suffice. If space is tight, a reading pillow—the kind that hugs your sides—would do the trick. Add a few velcro tabs, then apply a row of little stuffed animals onto each arm of the pillow!

AT SAMANTHA'S HOUSE

Samantha's mom, Debbie, promised herself that when she became a mom, she would never have "no touch" and "don't go there" zones in her home. It is much more important to her that Samantha enjoys their home.

It is obvious when you step into the home she shares with her daughter and husband that Debbie accomplished her goal. Each public room has comfortable seating and tasteful furnishings, but nothing feels contrived or "set up." Rather, there are nice antiques and rows of family photographs that express a cozy intimacy. The design attitude seems to say, "Sit here. Get comfy. Enjoy the view." That attitude continues in Samantha's little suite, which includes a bedroom, sitting room, and bath.

Debbie felt it was important for Samantha's growth and sense of self to have a place where she was comfortable and that she knew was hers. She started off in the room in her crib, and by the time she was two, she was in a double bed. When she is ill or feeling insecure, her mom soothes her in her own space and sometimes even sleeps next to her.

In anticipation of Samantha's arrival (her parents knew the baby was a girl), her mom and Mark, her dad, purchased the bed and crib and decided to decorate with a pink floral wallpaper. This caused some disagreement. Debbie wanted a yellow room, and Mark wanted a very feminine room with wallpaper.

"I wanted it to look like retro '50s, and he wanted it to be pink!" says Debbie. But Mark's interest in his new baby's room melted her heart, and the floral paper went up.

collection needed a home. At one point, a dollhouse was discussed, but Samantha's preference for inflatable chairs seemed like a nice decorating idea and suited her interests.

Some thoughtful design elements are worth noting in these rooms. For example, Samantha's bed is positioned in a corner between two big windows with seats instead of against an empty wall. She can climb into bed, look at the sky and mature trees to the left and right, and daydream. Curtains frame the window, and the valance punctuates the wonderful height.

Samantha is an avid dancer and quite concerned with her form—hence the mirror on a light wood stand at the foot of the bed. Another personal touch is the big chair next to the bed where the stuffed animals live. They all have names, and their proximity makes it convenient for Sam to grab one to join her for a nap or a chat. The chair's design and neutral color highlight the colorful pile of stuffed animals.

Nothing in here is fancy or untouchable. Samantha's parents have given her

They chose a simple, Shaker-style bed and, over time, added pertinent details as Samantha's interests developed. For example, the mirror at the foot of the bed lets her check her dance form. Likewise, the growing stuffed animal

the freedom to enjoy and organize the room to suit herself.

At one point, the sitting room was going to be a playroom, but Samantha really wanted it to be a place where she could sit and read. The lesson here is that once you begin a dialog with your children about their space, you can make discoveries that surprise and please you. Beyond that, you can work with your children to make a room a place they will use fully.

Samantha's sitting room is more like an adult's than a child's—except for two brightly colored inflatable chairs, where she reads and draws, and her doll collection (in the antique armoire). Another small doll collection sits on a wall shelf opposite the armoire, and a simple, low bookshelf is nearby.

That she loves the chairs is terrific, and that they are vinyl and easy to clean with a damp sponge is a benefit as well. Think about this kind of furniture for your children's spaces. It's durable, has no springs to wear out, and, having no fabric to stain, is easy to maintain.

For extra storage space in your child's room, consider using an armoire for

toys, books, clothes, or all three. The lower portion of Samantha's armoire holds towels and bathing suits. The little wall shelf is an example of a storage approach that adds color and texture to a room. Instead of dolls, put photos, a Beanie Babies collection, or even more books. You can purchase raw wood shelves and paint them or cover them with wallpaper.

A real life design success, Samantha's room is her sanctuary.

MATERIALS

Plush felt, 4 sheets, 18" x 22.5" (46 cm x 57 cm), I dark heather brown, 2 white, I light heather or tan

2 pillows, 16" (41 cm) square

Sticky-backed felt, 9" x 12" (23 cm x 30 cm), red, white, black

Six strand embroidery floss, 8.75 yd. (8 m), I black, I red

Polyester stuffing, 16 oz bag

Patterns (see pg. 98–99)

Sewing machine and thread

Hand-sewing needle

Embroidery needle

Scissors

Ruler

Light colored pencil (white or yellow)

CRAFTING WITH KIDS

PUPPY PILLOW TRIO

These three imaginative pillows brighten up a puppy-inspired decorating theme in a child's room. Easy patterns and simple shapes mean you can sew them in no time. And the appliqués are cut from sticky-back felt! The dog house and bone-shaped pillows are the perfect complement to the adorable black-and-white pup on the third pillow. You can easily follow the same steps using patterns you create to coordinate with the theme of your child's room.

INSTRUCTIONS

Dog bone pillow

1. Tape dog bone pattern piece 1 to pattern piece 2 as indicated on the patterns. Place the pattern on the folded white plush. Trace the pattern and cut out. This will yield two bones. Place the two pieces with right sides together (plush to plush), and sew from dot to dot, leaving an opening to stuff. Turn bone right side out, and stuff with polyester filling until plump. Slipstitch the remaining seam closed.

Doghouse pillow

1. Mark the doghouse pillow pattern. On the wrong side of the dark brown plush draw a 17" x 12" (43 cm x 30 cm) rectangle, using the light colored pencil so that the lines are clearly visible. On a long side, measure over 8.5" (22 cm), and mark the center with a notch. Repeat, making an identical rectangle on a second sheet of dark brown plush. Cut out each rectangle.

2. On the wrong side of the remaining piece of felt, draw two triangles that each measure 15" x 15" x 23" (38 cm x 38 cm x 58 cm). On the longest side, measure over 11.5" (29 cm), and mark the center with a notch. Cut out each triangle. Matching notches, sew each triangle to a rectangle using a .5" (1 cm) seam allowance.

3. With right sides together, sew the front of the doghouse to the back of the doghouse, leaving a 6" (15 cm) opening along the bottom edge. Turn the pillow right side out and stuff the triangle (the roof) with poly-fil. Insert a pillow form into the rectangle section and slip stitch the remaining seam closed. Where the triangle meets the rectangle, tie three quilter's tacks with the red embroidery floss. Trace the door patterns onto the red and the black felt. Trace the letters onto the white felt. Referring to the photograph for placement, peel back the paper, and place the door and the lettering on the pillow.

Puppy pillow

1. Cut out two 17" x 17" (43 cm x 43 cm) squares from the tan plush. With right sides together, sew along all edges, leaving a 6" (15 cm) opening along one side. Turn right side out and stuff the pillow with a pillow form. Slip stitch the remaining seam closed.

2. Trace the dog patterns onto the red, black, and white felt. Cut out the white dog. Peel the paper from the back of the felt, and place the dog in the center of the pillow. Cut out the red dog collar. Peel paper from the back of the felt, and place it around the dog's neck. Cut out the black eyes, nose, and two spots. Peel paper from the back of the felt, and place all the pieces as indicated by the illustration. Outline the entire dog by hand-sewing a blanket stitch with black embroidery thread.

TIPS

- Design a custom pillow that looks just like your pup. Use a favorite photograph as the basis for your pattern.

- Short Cuts: For a no-sew variation on these adorable pillows, glue felt shapes to ready made pillows. Or, outline pattern pieces on plain cotton pillow covers and color with textiles paints or crayons. Follow product instructions for setting colors.

PUPPY PILLOW TRIO PATTERNS

Photocopy at 167%

Photocopy at 200%

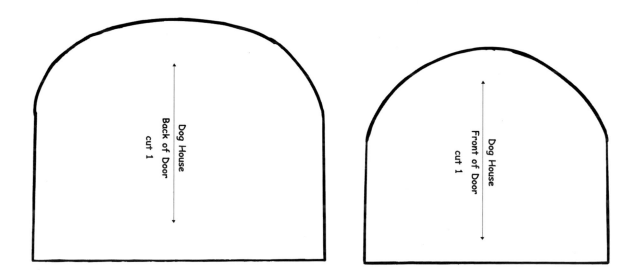

Decorating Kid's Rooms and Family-Friendly Spaces

Photocopy at 333%

Puppy Pillow
Placement Guide
Do Not Cut

Puppy Pillow
Dog Body cut 1

OO
Puppy Pillow
Eyes
cut 1

Puppy Pillow
Nose
cut 1

Puppy Pillow
Spot
cut 1

Puppy Pillow
Tail
cut 1

Puppy Pillow
Collar
cut 1

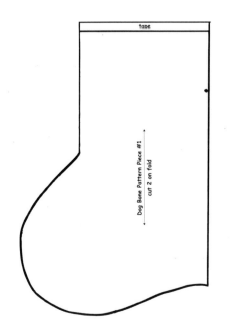

tape

Dog Bone Pattern Piece #1
cut 2 on fold

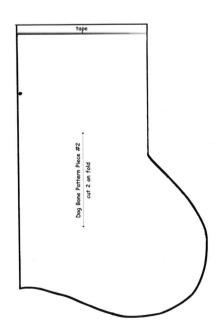

tape

Dog Bone Pattern Piece #2
cut 2 on fold

MATERIALS

Several Foam sheets, 2mm,
9" x 12" (23 cm x 30 cm),
in various colors

Dimensional fabric and
craft paint, in various colors

Broad point black
permanent marker

Scallop edge scissors

Pinking scissors

Regular edge scissors

Round hole punch

Opaque broad point pen, white

Blow dryer

Pen or pencil

SEASONAL PICTURE FRAMES

These picture frames are crafted out of colorful foam sheets,
an inexpensive medium that's easy to work with. Make several seasonal frames to decorate a wall of your child's room
with a progression of photos chronicling his growth over the
course of a year. Kids love to see how little they used to be.

INSTRUCTIONS

Autumn Frame

1. Cut out shapes. (See patterns, pages 102–103). With a pen or pencil, trace the pattern pieces onto the color foam sheets. Cut out the leaf shapes using pinking, regular, and scallop edge scissors.

2. Decorate shapes: Paint "veins" on the leaves with dimensional paint to match the color of the leaf. Set aside and let dry for 1 to 2 hours. Or, use a blow-dryer on a low setting to speed up the drying time.

3. Make the background. Using the scallop scissors, trim along the outside edges of all 4 sides of background color foam. Then, make dots all over the sheet with white dimensional paint. Let dry.

4. Attach photo to frame: Affix a photo to the center of the tan foam sheet by placing a small amount of tacky glue on the photo's edges. Arrange the leaves around the photo and glue in place.

TIP

Make a magnetic frame by adding an adhesive-back magnetic sheet to the tan foam. Simply peel the backing off the magnetic sheet and attach the magnet to the back part of the foam.

SEASONAL PICTURE FRAMES PATTERNS

Photocopy at 182%

Photocopy at 250%

Double Pumpkin

Photocopy at 182%

eyes/buttons

branches

nose

mitten

mitten

scarf

arm

GATHERING places

If any room is the epicenter of the household, it's the living room. It's where the most time is logged, and where the majority of a family's activities take place. In the old-fashioned salon, conversation was always at its best. Often the star room of a house, it is a wonderful place that evokes memories of laughter, holiday gatherings, cocktail hours, and Sunday-morning downtime. However, it can also be the home's noisy crossroads—where homework is done, last-minute plans are made, and impromptu wrestling matches are decided. An overcrowded war room at its worst and a comfortable, utilitarian haven at its best, the living room must serve many purposes if it is to accomodate your family well.

OPPOSITE A window seat is a great way to fill a window nook. With a custom-fit, upholstered cushion and a few soft pillows, a window seat can provide both a cozy reading area and extra seating for guests. The extra shelves underneath for storage are useful, too.

designs that meet everyone's needs

To start, take all of the family's needs into consideration. What is your living room used for? Who uses it most? When do they use it? If these needs overlap, try to be creative about accommodating as many of them as possible. Can you create separate seating areas within the room? Can you give these seating areas separate light sources so the light level can be flexible for each? A couch and armchairs around a coffee table can occupy one end of the room and accommodate socializing, TV watching, and board games, while a table with chairs and a brighter overhead light sits at the other end and can be used for homework. Screens can partition off spaces from visual distraction. As a last resort, headphones can come in handy if, for instance, one child simply must watch a particular TV show while another needs to practice at the piano. It may take some careful thought, but with planning, multipurpose living rooms can work.

LEFT Sleek, low sofas are paired with floor cushions for a relaxed attitude in this family's living room. A knotted-wool area rug leaves a comfortable play area, and high book-shelves display objects, photos, and books out of harm's way.

STYLE FILE: family photos

Photographs make a home your own by imbuing it with your family's own style and flair. Each photo keeps a loved one present or tells a story of a trip or holiday that your family spent together.

Black-and-white photographs blend seamlessly into any living room's decor. Vintage sepia-toned family photos and wedding portraits add meaning and a historical touch. Recent color photos of your children are always appropriate. Stylish details, like framing and placement, should be considered as carefully as any other element in the living room. Sterling-silver frames, painted rustic wood, or silver-gilt can give formal or fun touches to a living room without overdoing it. Various ready-made frames are available, as are flip-book stands and beautiful photo albums.

Photographs can be artfully arranged on a wall or clustered together in a cheerful crowd. They can be placed on a coffee table, propped on the shelf of a bookcase, or sprinkled judiciously in nooks around the living room. A few can sit atop a mantle, alongside other objects, such as candlesticks, a bud vase, or a collection of Murano glass. Or, if you prefer, you can devote an entire wall of the living room to family photographs that have been framed to dot the walls like art. Use the same-style frames for a unified look, and then group them together on the wall.

Arrange photos by theme or according to a specific time line. Create a small vignette by placing a photograph of a family trip to Europe next to an object acquired there. The vignette will tell a story every time it catches your eye. Group pictures of your children's graduations from kindergarten and grade school together, leaving room to add other photos in the future. Heirloom photographs, too, are a special way to display family history.

Your particular memories that have been so carefully recorded and preserved add a wonderful touch to a living room's style. Whether a tiny detail shot or a whole series of pictures from the latest family vacation, photographs can personalize the room in a unique way.

DISPLAYING FAMILY PHOTOGRAPHS

- Group photographs together on the wall above the sofa or mantel to make them the focal point of the room.
- Add souvenirs and vintage photos to a family room, as a way of keeping family history alive.
- Use black-and-white pictures for a monochromatic palette that seamlessly blends into a neutral decor.
- Hang photos at eye level, line them horizontally, or group them closely on one wall. There are no rules—go with whatever works best for you.
- Frames with interesting details can add glamour to a room without being extravagant. Choose frames made of silver, covered with leather, or wrapped in an exotic skin like alligator or shagreen.

the formal living room

Just as the living room is an important a place for family, it may also be the prime space for entertaining guests. However, sophisticated looks don't have to be stiff. Art and chic furniture can easily be mixed together for a living room that works for the entire family during the day, and transforms into an intimate setting for cocktails and conversation at night.

If your living room is the room for entertaining, it should be on the formal side. Keep in mind, however, it is possible to combine style with function. Sturdy twill is a good choice for covering sofas. It is resilient enough to withstand a lot of wear, and it can be easily washed, especially if it's in slipcover form. Another option that combines easy maintenance

with style is a woven floor treatment like a sisal or sea-grass rug. The natural textures are neutral enough to work in a variety of rooms and are no longer considered beach-house decor. They can be used in minimalist, pared-down rooms just as easily as in the most rococo of salons. Best of all, they are fairly inexpensive and durable, and they clean up easily with a good vacuum. An Oriental rug is another viable option for your floors. It can add a great deal of warmth and comfort underfoot, and if it is dark colored and patterned, it can hide a multitude of sins. Although you will want to stow away the heirloom rugs for when the kids are almost grown, a good-quality wool oriental is worth the investment.

BELOW To create a chic-yet-livable living room, cover a sofa in off-white twill, add colorful graphic pillows, and finish it off with a pair of funky, vintage armchairs. Black-and-white photographs on the wall add an elegant touch.

OPPOSITE In this living room, dark wood and velvet uphol-stery project a coolly sophisticated look against a canvas of neutral walls. Placing a traditional rug like this one in the center adds warmth and encourages flopping on the floor for games or reading.

Kid-friendly Formality

Creating a formal living room doesn't mean that kids can't feel at home there, too. Cotton and wool are good fabric choices for upholstered furniture because they are easy to clean (just be sure the fabric has been treated with a protective, stain-resistant coating), are sturdy enough to withstand trampoline practice every now and then when you aren't looking, and look good in any color. Keep in mind that both solid, light colors and solid, dark colors show spills and grime easily and are best avoided unless used as washable slipcovers. Leather is another good choice for upholstery because it is very durable and, unless it is the sleek modern black or beige variety, it will even gain character with wear and tear. Low tables of varying heights encourage activity and a casual atmosphere where sitting on the floor is allowed. Even if chic enough to host the most formal of gatherings, a room doesn't have to scream, "Don't touch." Elements of warmth lend an inviting air—overstuffed cushions, roomy seating, soft throws, and a few plants create a comfortable atmosphere. A sprinkling of books never hurts, either.

Open space is essential for entertaining. It gives guests a chance to mingle and stretch their legs. However, ample seating is also important. Window seats along the corners of a living room provide extra spots that don't crowd floor space, double as separate reading nooks, and maintains the room's serious air.

Mantelpieces offer an opportunity to display something beautiful, whether it's a collection of china, jewel-toned Murano glass, or family photographs. Often serving as the focal point for a room, the mantelpiece is a place where you can showcase objects at a height safe from harm.

SHOPPING: sofas

Let's face it: Most of the time that your family spends in the living room is spent on the sofa. Whether for lounging and daydreaming, reading a novel, eating a light snack, or just watching television, the sofa is the most-used piece of furniture in the room. It needs to be comfortable, resilient, and attractive enough to serve as the room's centerpiece. Buying a sofa merits deliberation. The good news is that with so many options on the market, it shouldn't be difficult to choose the one that works best for your living room and lifestyle.

SOFA OPTIONS AND CONSIDERATIONS

When studying sofas, take note of dimensions. First of all, figure out the size of the biggest sofa that will fit in its allotted space. It's important that it not be dwarfed by a big space or dominate an area that's too small. And it must accommodate lots of family members all at once. For comfort, the depth and seat height of a sofa are key. Roomy sofas that can accommodate long legs—and even an entire family—are usually the deeper ones. But you may not want it so deep that you need a tow rope to climb out. Make sure you test drive before buying so your sofa is deep and tall enough for you and your family to be comfortable. Don't forget the necessity of soft cushions. Overstuffed sofas with lots of pillows and thick cushions also add a comfortable element. Realize that if you have young children, and you choose a sofa with a back made of separate pillows rather than one upholstered piece, the pillows may land on the floor frequently, usually to serve as a fort. If this bothers you, choose the more tailored, upholstered back. Details like the height of the back and the style of the arms are also important. Perhaps a high back might be too rigid for you; a low back might not seem cozy. You might prefer rounded or scrolled arms for a little extra padding, or more angular edges for a streamlined look. And it's worth it to pay a little more for firmer cushions. Foam cushions won't take the abuse children mete out. Pay attention to the details when searching for the ultimate sofa—they'll make a difference.

Fabric

Given all the activity it's expected to withstand, a sofa fabric should be strong to stand the test of time. Look for fabrics that are stain-resistant and washable, preferably by machine. A pristine, white sofa may look great at first, but it will require frequent cleaning. Opt for what's reasonable, low-maintenance, and still attractive. Keep in mind that lighter colors and solid dark colors require more maintenance because dirt and lint show up more easily. Twill and sturdy cottons can get lots of mileage in any hue for sofa upholstery, as can good-quality velvet, wool, and heavy felts. Consider a pattern in a bold color like red or deep maroon. Not only will it be attractive and make a statement, it will also prove less work than a light-colored fabric. Machine-washable slipcovers, rather than custom-upholstery, are another quality to look for in a sofa. They can be regularly washed for upkeep and are relatively inexpensive to change if you tire of a color or pattern. Leather, which gets softer and achieves a modulated, worn look with age, also works as a low-maintenance upholstery. Although once considered off-limits for its tendency to stain, new forms of machine-washable and stain-resistant ultrasuede can be used on sofas, too.

Make sure you like what you're buying as you'll use your sofa everyday. Never buy a piece furniture that you're unsure about. It is possible to find a sofa that is low-maintenance and comfortable, and will look polished and clean.

SOFA-SHOPPING CHECKLIST

- Bring a measuring tape! Make sure the sofa fits in the required space and through doorways.
- Pick a fabric that can stand wear and tear.
- Test drive before you buy! Sit down, stretch out, and relax before making a decision. Remember: You'll be spending lots of time here.
- Color is the easiest way to make a design statement in a room, whether it be a neutral tone; a bright, bold color; or a graphic pattern that can capture a child's imagination.
- Make sure the sofa fits the location. Proportions are key: Small-scale furniture in a small room can make it look even smaller. Conversely, oversized pieces in a large room don't necessarily fill up the space.
- Add a variety of textures to the sofa, with accessories such as soft wool or mohair throws, or pillows dressed up in cashmere. Small touches like these help make a room cozy and family-friendly.

the family room

From the most grandiose to the humblest of family rooms, comfort and versatility are key. A family room is a place where families can work, play, nap, and even dine now and then. It's a room where the family can convene and relax over any number of activities at once.

Although books and games are important to a modern family's leisure time, the TV is indisputably the primary form of entertainment for most families these days. If you prefer to limit TV watching, you can keep the set out of sight in a cabinet or in one of the many attractive armoires designed specifically for entertainment equipment. But if you accept that the TV plays an important role in your family's life, there's no need to hide it. Simply integrate it into your stylish decor. After all, TVs aren't as ugly as they used to be. And attractive, wall-mounted options like plasma-screen TVs are now available. Although expensive, these TVs free up floor space and eliminate clunky cords and wires so your children can play safely nearby. But if a plasma set isn't in your budget, try placing the television on a stand or table with stylish touches surrounding it. Pictures, flowers, or beautiful artifacts from your travels can be just as enticing here as anywhere else in the family room.

Designs That Convey Fun

In most homes, the family room is where low maintenance meets style, and so many different elements go into creating it, from books and games, to televisions and stereos, to key pieces of furniture, such as sofas, tables, and bookcases. It's an area that should have open spaces and invite relaxation. A pool table, like the one shown in the family room at the right, sets the tone for an informal space where games are meant to be played and fun is meant to be had. A pool table is a great draw for teenagers in particular, but if billiards isn't your style, you can just as easily have a table-tennis or air-hockey table—whatever suits you. A seat at the base of the stone fireplace adds relaxed seating to a room that would be equally comfortable hosting children or adults at play. (Notice the curved corners of the stone hearth that help reduce the danger of bumps and bruises when small children are around.) The tomes lining the bookcase also suggest that a family room can support quiet time as well. The room should be furnished with comfortable sofas, resilient fabrics, and smaller tables. Or, you can go without furniture to create a large, open space for play. Whether your children enjoy puzzles, blocks, or cars and racetracks, the floor is the space of choice for any number of such activities, especially when the children are small.

Open space and simple settings are equally viable as a room that's chockfull of electronic and gaming equipment. In a well-designed family room seen on page 52, there's room to pursue both daydreams and prime-time dreams, providing fertile ground for young imaginations. The throws on the sofa suggest that this room is for relaxing—and that napping is encouraged.

ABOVE A stone hearth and book-lined, wooden shelves create a multitude of textures and a cozy atmosphere in this family room. Comfortable upholstery in light, airy fabrics softens a game room entrenched in stone like this one. But don't forget room for play. Leave space for items like this pool table.

Vacation Home Family Rooms

Vacation homes, like any other type of home, also need casual, multipurpose family rooms. A rainy day when you're on vacation is twice as bad if children don't have enough room to play. Leave room in cabinets for storing games and puzzles. Furniture can be covered in lightweight cottons, and printed fabrics can be placed around the room, adding cheerful jolts of color. Director's chairs add inexpensive extra seating, while adding a nautical motif.

ABOVE The clearing in this family room, framed by the bucolic view through a large picture window, leaves a space worthy of imagination and allows ample room for play. Place simple chairs at either corner for extra seating that can easily be cleared for more room. A multicolored rug pulls this room together and helpfully disguises lint and dust.

OPPOSITE Classic nautical stripes set the casual tone in this family room. The white-painted rafters add informality to the dramatic ceilings and views, and the low, fabric-covered coffee table is big enough to accommodate games and puzzles. Kids will love to explore the seashells placed on the window ledge. Touches like these bring a bit of the outdoors in.

KID-FRIENDLY: fabrics

To accommodate the traffic of the living room, sturdy fabrics are needed. For the best results, upholstery should be a durable, heavy weave, easy to clean, and no-fuss. Other fabrics that work include twill, heavy-woven cotton, wool, felt, and leather in darker colors that have been stain-proofed. Patterns need less upkeep than solids, but the rest of the fabrics in the living room should follow suit. From window treatments to carpets to pillows, all of the living room's touches can be durable and still look sophisticated.

WINDOW TREATMENTS

Although not directly involved in most of the living room's action, the window treatments should still be considered fair game. You'll be surprised how they, too, can become targets for stains or spills. Blinds are an option to consider. Whether wood or aluminum, most require just an easy dusting to keep clean and are simple enough for any of your children to operate. They're resilient, too. Most blinds last a lifetime. But always be careful not to leave the cords hanging when small children might be in the room alone. Although more difficult to manage, curtains can still be had in the living room. Billowing silk curtains that hang to the floor or delicate and filmy gauze can be beautiful, but these may require more frequent cleaning. Consider heavy-duty cotton or darker colors. A shorter curtain that hangs to just the window instead of to the floor can be easier to deal with as well. Although less dramatic, they're easier to keep clean and less tempting to young fingers (or to hide-and-seek players). Remember: You want your living room to be played in and enjoyed, and not full of hands-off areas for your children.

FLOORING

Flooring also requires lots of consideration. If you're lucky enough to have hardwood floors in your home, you are a step ahead in the style department. They're not only beautiful but also easy to maintain. Just make sure you protect them by keeping them clean and putting felt protectors on the legs of chairs. An area rug will beautify any type of flooring, with low-pile or natural rugs being the easiest to maintain. Sisal, sea grass, or jute rugs come in natural tones that complement almost any room, and are available in dyed versions if you want a dose of color. Short-pile or flat, woven-wool rugs are also easy to maintain and come in a wide range of colors and patterns. For an ethnic vibe, flat-woven dhurries release dirt easily and are as easy to maintain as any natural floor covering. But if your heart is set on an Oriental rug, don't despair. Although you may want to put away the antique one until the kids are out of toddlerhood, a less-precious Oriental carpet can be quite durable. Simply stick with one-hundred percent wool, and give it a stain-resistant treatment.

OPPOSITE   In this living room, dark wood and velvet uphol-stery project a sophisticated look against a canvas of neutral walls. Try placing a traditional rug in the center to create a cozy atmosphere.

ACCESSORIES

In the rest of the living room, pay attention to the accents, too. Pillows and throws should be pretty, but not necessarily precious. Delicate silk or light-colored fabrics are best reserved for a room that isn't used as often. But if you've been holding out on color for big items like sofas and walls, you can add that splash of intense color with your pillows or other decorations.

If you keep to fabrics sturdy enough for the rigors of family life, you'll have ample room for plenty of style so that your children can play undisturbed and your entire family can be comfortable for years to come in a stylish and easy-to-maintain living space.

KID-FRIENDLY FABRICS

- Machine-washable fabrics are always the best choice for slipcovers, curtains, and throw rugs.
- Cotton, twill, felt, and wool upholstery fabrics are easy to keep clean and can last a lifetime.
- If using leather, soften the look with velvet or cashmere pillows or a soft throw.
- Curtain fabric should be considered, too! Like upholstery, make sure it's resilient and easy to clean.
- Floor treatments in highly trafficked areas can be stylish and easily maintained. Try sisal, sea grass, or low-pile wool.
- Antique rugs and other precious heirloom fabrics aren't off-limits. Just make sure they're treated for stain resistance.
- Don't forget comfort! Soft throws and cozy pillows lend an inviting touch and are more comfortable for children to lounge on when reading or watching TV.
- Plants and greenery inject life into a room and help make the air healthier for the family to breathe.

the multipurpose room

Living rooms so often serve several purposes: a family room, a room in which to entertain, and a playroom. Paradoxically, for a family short on space, accommodating all the family's needs is easier if the room itself is simple. More functions don't have to mean more furniture. Versatility is key when it comes to combining needs in a single room. But how do you combine a living room, playroom, and even possibly an office into one space without the clutter?

Incorporating a Home Office

A corner of a room can easily be converted into an office space large enough for a desk, and still leave room for the usual living room pieces and allow activity to flow unimpeded. If you house the computer in an armoire, it can easily be concealed when you entertain guests. Whether you have a stand-alone desk or a storage unit, if you want your office furniture to be unobtrusive, choose it from a palette similar to the rest of the room. If the room is a white on-white space, a neutral or white-toned desk would blend in best. Similarly, antique mahogany pieces are perfect for a darker color scheme. The more difficult task is preserving enough play area for children. Ideally, large, open spaces are best, but with sofas, desks, and other furniture already populating the room, the space can be crowded. Eliminating the coffee table and using only side tables next to the sofa can create larger, open areas for play. Cabinets, bookshelves, or roomy armoires will add plenty of shelving for storing and organizing toys and other games kept in the living room. Armoires or chests with drawers are a great option for a modified toy bin, and still provide shelves for video games, books, DVDs, and the like.

Stackable bookshelves are also extremely useful. If necessary, another set of shelves can be added for more room, or they can be dismantled easily and moved elsewhere. Office furniture stores as well as home furnishings shops offer inexpensive bookcases that work by themselves or combine with several others to create a shelving system. If you use your living room for entertaining, try to find units with doors or drawers that shut so you can keep toys out of sight during adult time.

Maximizing Space

If you don't want to give up the coffee table to maximize floor space, use minimal furniture with a softened palette to allow movement and comfort. Leather club chairs piled with soft throws and cushions are as comfortable as an overstuffed sofa. Baskets underneath the coffee table can serve as storage for toys and games. Use an ottoman as a coffee table to eliminate hazardous sharp corners; it can fill in as extra seating if a crowd shows up. A low-maintenance carpet provides a padded area for a play space. Different textures, a variety of tones, and integrated furniture all come together to make a living room work to fulfill various needs.

ORGANIZING: storage solutions

Living rooms are meant for living. Living requires stuff, but not as much stuff as we usually manage to accumulate, so storage becomes a necessity in most family rooms. Try to plan for it. Items that tend to amass in the high-traffic living room include toys, books, videos, and magazines. Many other objects also find a temporary home here. But with a few additions of storage space, your living room can remain relatively clutter free.

In many homes, the living room is the media and entertainment center of the household, and that means CDs, DVDs, and video games inevitably end up there. Bookcases and racks made expressly for storing CDs can do the trick, but if you have small children, try to find closable racks or units that can be placed out of their reach. Toddlers love to empty shelves. Bookcases can hold family photos and other decorative accents, as well as books and media equipment. If you need additional space, stacked Lucite cubes or wall shelves near the stereo can help organize your collection without adding clutter. Small, stacking bookcases are ideal for smaller spaces, too. As objects accumulate, you can add another shelf or unit, building upward to save valuable floor space. Make sure tall furniture is stable, though. If not built in, it's best to bolt tall bookcases and bureaus to the wall. For televisions, it may be best to invest in an armoire or a media unit, complete with its own shelves and drawers to house the necessary accessories. Although many armoires are specifically designed to store entertainment systems, others can be modified to allow for electronics.

OPPOSITE A boldly patterned rug is the centerpiece in this airy living room. Narrow shelves are tucked in at the corners, alongside window seats, adding storage space and unobtrusive seating spaces.

STORAGE TIPS

· Try to combine function with form: a table that doubles as a storage trunk or a window seat that also encloses storage space can work wonders.

· Hang single shelves on a wall to display decorative objects without compromising floor space.

· Use colorful boxes and baskets to give the room style while doubling as storage space for magazines and other odds and ends.

· Be creative in finding storage solutions: under a coffee table, in an armoire, perhaps even in baskets under the couch.

· Bookshelves and étagères are great ways to display books and objects. Use the higher shelves to hold valuable items and the lower shelves to hold the children's books and toys.

· An armoire or console can be a versatile piece of furniture. Make sure when purchasing one that it can fulfill all your needs.

· Seating is important to a room. Try to add comfortable places to sit by adding cushions to a window seat or piling large floor pillows in a corner.

A smaller bookshelf, a corner étagère, or a wall shelf in a bright color or an unusual design can create an interest point as well as add storage space. It's also nice to keep extra throw pillows, coverlets, board games, and puzzles at hand. Before overstuffing the existing bookcases, consider some other options. Storage trunks can easily double as side or coffee tables, housing board games that are rarely used, extra pillows or blankets that help transition a room from spring to winter, and other rarely used items. They'll be out of sight, but still accessible, if needed. Two-tiered tables are another possibility. Add baskets below for greater organization. A few magazines, books, or even toys can be stashed in them, providing easy access. Attractive, stacked boxes or baskets can serve the same purpose.

Magazine racks or baskets can also give a stylish or daring touch to a living room. Wall-mounted or standing racks take up little room, but they can provide lots of storage space. For a rustic touch and an easy place to stow toys during cleanup, consider scattering baskets around the living area. A quick sweep is all it takes to tidy up for evening guests.

KITCHENS

Varying in size, style, and purpose, the kitchen is often considered the linchpin of the house. From the centuries-old image of a crackling hearth that drew family members to the belly of the house to the modern-day snacking stop and message center, the kitchen remains as a primetime space for everyone. Whether you're cooking, entertaining, or just simply eating, it's likely that a family-friendly kitchen has requirements to fill such as safety, storage, and function.

RIGHT: Draw your family together by making your kitchen serve several functions at once—workstation, eating area, and chef's quarters. Provide plenty of seating, like these wood-and-stainless steel bar stools. Mix stainless-steel surfacing with brick walls for a sophisticated yet warm effect. A small-screen television discreetly perched above the refrigerator serves its function without cluttering the kitchen work area.

your kitchen's purpose

Food is literally sustenance for living and as such, brings families together, day after day. Whether it's a quick snack or an elaborate dinner, there's never a day that the kitchen isn't put to use. Food is love, or as M.F.K. Fisher said even more eloquently: "It seems to me that our three basic needs, for food and security and love, are so mixed and mingled and entwined that we cannot straightly think of one without the others. So it happens that when I write of hunger, I am really writing about love and the hunger for it." Naturally, a dark, unwelcoming kitchen is one of the first places that you would begin revamping for your family.

A well-organized kitchen doesn't necessarily mean top-of-the line appliances and all the amenities. As in any other room in the house, the ideal decor is what works best for you and your family. Stainless steel and bleached wood are both attractive and modern, but stylish kitchens come in every variety. Colorful wood, lots of tchotchkes, and mismatched place mats work just as well for streamlined living, as long as the kitchen is well organized. If you're an accomplished chef, it's probably necessary for you to have high-quality machinery and utensils. But if you're strictly cooking the most elementary basics, that's fine too; maybe the sparsest collection of pots and pans will suffice. Anything goes.

Because the kitchen often doubles as a dining area, it may also be important to consider which meals are served there. If only breakfast and snacks are consumed in the kitchen, an informal daytime decor serves the purpose. If dinner in the kitchen is a regular habit, you may want to consider a more versatile style that transforms easily from a casual lunch spot to a serene setting for evening dining for the entire family, as well as a guest or two. For instance, you'll want to fit in a table and chairs rather than just stools at a counter, and shades rather than bare windows will make the kitchen feel cozier at night.

If your kitchen opens onto the living room and transforms into a party room when you entertain, a kitchen island can do double duty as a bar for serving cocktails, and still be childproof and safe for the children to roam around during the day. If you entertain often, you may want to consider putting in an extra oven, an extra-large refrigerator, and lots of storage areas, because advance preparation is key to managing a dinner party and family life at the same time.

OPPOSITE Although kitchens aren't normally play areas, the occasional scoot-by is allowed en route to the outdoor patio of this house. Place crystal vases and bowls out of reach but visible to add a glamorous effect. A farmhouse-style wooden table paired with sturdy, functional modern chairs immediately makes this kitchen a comfortable place for family dining or casual entertaining.

ORGANIZING: design basics

Creating order in the kitchen seems like making method out of madness in some cases, but a well-organized kitchen can transform the cooking experience from chaos to pleasure. Use your space creatively. Whether you have a pantry or just a few cabinets, you'll be surprised at how much mileage you can get out of your storage space.

Even the smallest and most mundane spaces can serve as storage room. Pretty vases, bowls, or glass can be stored atop cabinets that don't reach all the way to the ceiling. Kitchen islands or butcher blocks with a lower tier can hold items too, as long as they aren't items that would be dangerous to children. Make sure no space is left unturned. Sometimes additional shelving can be added to existing cabinets to increase surface space. Faux drawers under the sink can even be transformed into a shallow, pivoting drawer to hold a sponge or utensils. Cabinets with shelves that slide out can keep cookware, especially stacked pots and pans or baking dishes, easily accessible. If you don't already have a cabinet over the refrigerator, consider adding one.

PANTRY POLISH

- Store food or other objects in an interesting way—in empty mason jars or other glass vessels.
- Add overhead pot racks to free up valuable storage space and make the kitchen more attractive, especially if you have polished copper pots.
- Store frequently used utensils in easy-to-reach jars to free up storage space elsewhere.
- Use the often-forgotten under-sink area, too!
- Look for inefficiently used spaces where you could add shelves, racks, or drawers.
- Install glass cabinets in the kitchen so the whole family can find things easily. Even young kids can fix themselves breakfast if you keep cereal, bowls, and spoons on the lower shelves in those cabinets.
- Don't forget to add a message board: The kitchen is often the family's communication center.

OPPOSITE A versatile, chrome storage rack like this one can be placed along a wall to increase pantry space. The butcher block on top of the smaller rack adds an extra work surface too. If your rack has wheels, make sure they lock in place so that children can't move it when they're playing.

the family-friendly kitchen

No matter the size, shape, or design, every family kitchen must have a common denominator, and that is safety. It's important for children to be aware of safety precautions and to learn rudimentary kitchen no-nos. And when decorating, it's important for you to consider safety details such as flooring that isn't too slick, tables with rounded corners, and surfaces that are durable enough for kids to use. Some safety considerations are obvious, like keeping knives and cleaning liquids out of the reach of toddlers, but look through your pediatrician's child-proofing guidelines as you design your kitchen to be sure you don't overlook anything.

Ideally, the kitchen shouldn't double as a playroom, but the irresistible charm of baking cookies draws everyone in the house into the kitchen. And who minds having company in the kitchen? Just make sure you can navigate with ease and without tripping over toys. Again, the key to a kitchen that can successfully hold the entire family lies in its safety and organization.

OPPOSITE For a workstation that doubles as a seating area, use an extended kitchen island like this one, where cheerful yellow stools provide easy seating for baking cookies or conversation. For children's stools, make sure they're set off at the corner, away from dangerous appliances.

ABOVE For added storage, line shelves and drawers up an entire wall, like those in this whitewashed kitchen. Fragile glasses and containers are placed on high shelves, and durable books and bowls are within everyone's reach. Floral plates are hung on the wall to add a delicate touch, and an expandable, white-painted kitchen table gives a bit of practical savoir faire.

Carve Out Cooking and Eating Areas

A safe kitchen can still be stylish and comfortable. Farmhouse-style kitchen furnishings, built with durability in mind, can work in numerous hues and settings. If your taste runs more to modern style, stainless steel and stone can be made warmer with a few splashes of color. Stylish details can add flair to any kitchen, either sparingly or boldly.

The goal of making the kitchen a family-friendly spot can be helped by separating cooking and eating areas. Besides providing a built-in spot for impromptu dining, a kitchen island also gives the chef valuable work space; just remember to keep seats away from the stove and knives and cutting boards away from the seating area. If there's room, an informal table is one of the best ways to accommodate family time in the kitchen. It's also lovely to have an armchair or sofa in the kitchen to encourage family members to lounge while you cook. If you have small children, try to avoid using upholstered chairs at the table—keeping them clean is a hopeless task. If your dining room is on the formal side, have fun with the kitchen eating area. Bright colors look great and feel welcoming to children; let loose a little with bright, eye-popping hues, or, if you prefer, stick to a toned-down palette to encourage order and calm.

ABOVE Add friendly jolts of color to the kitchen with a window-seat bench outfitted with a striped cushion and loads of colorful pillows. For added effect, paint only a border or trim, like these cobalt-blue window frames that contrast with the wooden chairs and white furniture and add definition to the room.

KID-FRIENDLY: heavy-duty surfaces

Kitchen surfaces inevitably take lots of abuse, which is why they should be durable above all. Fortunately, many options are available, so kitchen surfaces can be resilient, family-friendly, and stylish all at once. By changing these surfaces, you can also update the entire look of your kitchen. Materials vary widely in price, however. Try to strike a balance between the best-looking, most functional, and most durable surface of your dreams and the right price.

STAINLESS STEEL

Stainless steel combines gleaming looks and professional-quality utilitarianism. Previously, it was used primarily in commercial kitchens, but its stark look can be softened by using wood for cabinets or furniture and by adding other homey details. Not only does it look polished, stainless steel is also extremely resilient. Stainless steel never stains or burns, making it a perfect child-safe surface in that respect. However, it does require constant cleaning—fingerprints are forever visible if it isn't pristine. But beware of the cost—it's an expensive material.

ABOVE For a coolly sharp kitchen that's still soft, consider wood. In this kitchen—with ceilings, cabinets, and a low kitchen table made of wood—a saunalike effect is created. The textured warmth of the wood softens the sleek, modern look, and the low benches lend a welcoming feel, inviting children to slide in. The backsplash tiles and linoleum work surfaces add a touch of practicality, as they are both washable and durable.

CORIAN SOLID SURFACES

Corian, a trademarked composite made by DuPont, is a technologically advanced surface material made of resins and minerals that can be shaped into any surface. Cuts or scratches can be sanded down like a wood surface, and it's extremely easy to maintain. The range of colors offered is extensive. Colors like apple green or intense blue-lavender are sure to make any kitchen pop. More conservative granite or marbled looks can be had if your taste runs on the quieter side.

CERAMIC SURFACES

Ceramic tiles are another alternative, and they come in a multitude of colors, sizes, and patterns. Unlike monochromatic stainless seal or Corian surfaces, tiles allow the option of creating a decorative pattern. Pick tiles within the same color family to give surfaces a weathered, imperfect look, or put together a rainbow of colors if you prefer a colorful, offbeat aesthetic. With tiles you can get more creative. They can also be finished with a paint sealant to protect them and make them easier to clean. Although tiles are resilient, be careful while chopping because even the strongest tiles can chip.

NATURAL MATERIALS

Natural materials such as wood, granite, or marble can make attractive surface materials, but as a whole, they're a bit more fragile. Wood surfaces naturally change over time, becoming weathered and scratched through everyday wear. But wood can also be treated with sealant to make it more durable, and it may fit the style and decor that you're aiming for. Granite and marble (like slate, limestone, and other stone tops) are much more resistant to scratches, but they are susceptible to stains. Unlike wood, they can't be sanded down and may be bit more fragile if used in large sheets.

HEAVY-DUTY SURFACES

- Flooring and surfaces should be stylish but not too slippery; make sure your children can navigate easily.

- Consider the costs of all the options; they can differ dramatically.

- Realistically assess your kitchen use before deciding; the needs of a professional chef are different from those of an average household cook.

- Whether you opt for metal, marble, or wood, each can completely alter the look of your kitchen; therefore, once you choose the surface that best meets your needs, keep to your color palette for a more cohesive look.

- Easy-to-clean surfaces are a must in a high-activity kitchen. When children are around, countertops, floors, walls, chairs, and tables will all need frequent scrubbing. Avoid white floors.

- Add color on the counters or the floors if you want dramatic results.

ABOVE Although the actual kitchen in this house can fit only a small, round table, the dining nook alongside holds a wide, solid table that accommodates everything from a big family dinner to art projects. The zinc sheeting in the middle of the table can take much abuse, and the roomy benches had a prior life as church pews.

135

Make the Most of Awkward or Small Spaces

Although big, roomy kitchens are wonderful, in cities and smaller vacation homes in particular, kitchens are often compressed into one small space in which appliances, dishes, foodstuffs, and all the accoutrements of cooking must fit. When thinking small, don't also think dull and utilitarian. Small kitchens can still be welcoming family spaces with bright colors and accents, and proximity to comfortable seating. Additional storage like an armoire in the dining area can accommodate cooking utensils. If the space is seriously tiny and lacking in sunlight, consider opening it up to the rest of the house. Knocking down a wall can drastically improve the appearance of the room—as well as broadcast to the family that this space is not only for eating but also for relaxing.

In loft spaces where the kitchen is already just a nook off of the living room, there's no need to demolish any walls, but perhaps you want to section off the kitchen into its own area. Solution? Paint that area its own color, or mark the beginning of the kitchen with a large cabinet or other piece of furniture. Or, if you want to keep the room monochromatic, you can use screens to create room divisions, which, as a bonus, provide a place to pin up your children's artwork. It's also possible that simply the placement of the kitchen's appliances and furniture can provide enough separation.

Space restrictions shouldn't put a limit on your style. With a bit of ingenuity, a small space can get lots of mileage. Judicious use of color and thoughtful use of space can transform any kitchen from the purely functional into a family-ready, central location where meals can be prepared, homework can be done, and cookies can be baked.

ABOVE In this vacation-house duplex, the kitchen's open plan gives the illusion of a larger space. As a result, the counter bar with bar chairs becomes a gathering place for the family. The glass cabinets stock colorful dinnerware and decorative objects.

ABOVE To brighten up a small, dark kitchen, paint it taxicab yellow. Ordinary veneer cabinets with updated handles take on an altogether different look next to the cheery color. Brushed-aluminum lamps, fifties-style chairs, and the family's flea market finds help energize the space.

safety in a working kitchen

"The more, the merrier" is an adage that we've advocated for the kitchen, but how can all this fun be had while serious cooking takes place? Organization is the key to a viable kitchen that belongs to both chef and children. Although adults likely do most of the cooking in the kitchen, it shouldn't be considered an all-adult domain. Teach your children about kitchen safety. They should know what the different appliances are and any necessary safety precautions. If they're old enough to learn how to use some of the kitchen's devices, make sure they can use them properly and with caution. Careless accidents are common in the kitchen, but many are easily preventable. It's particularly important to keep the paths clear between the major work spaces: stove, sink, refrigerator, and countertops. Make sure you can you get a pot of boiling water from stove to sink without having to negotiate obstacles. If you have toddlers and infants just learning to crawl and walk, consider setting up a safety zone. Use high chairs, safety gates, and playpens, and situate them away from appliances. Keep stools and chairs away from the stove so that inquisitive toddlers can't climb up.

Pots and pans must be easily accessible for a working chef. Hanging them on the wall or from the ceiling on a pot rack clears out lower cabinets and shelves and keeps heavy pots out of children's reach. Favorite utensils should be easily accessible. Pretty ceramics or jars can store spatulas, spoons, and ladles to help eliminate last-minute searches in a cluttered drawer. Knives can be hung on a wall, out of reach of small fingers. Some chefs like to display dry goods in glass containers. Pearly white rice grains, long strands of spaghetti, and viscous olive oil can look sculptural when displayed on a kitchen counter or in glass cabinets. Open counter space for chopping and food preparation is a must. Small appliances that are used often should also be kept close by.

OPPOSITE Put a storage unit next to your kitchen table so kids can do everything from artwork to board games while you cook; these things can be quickly swept away when dinner is ready. White paint, high ceilings, and brightly colored accents keep this kitchen area bright and welcoming, even without many windows.

SHOPPING: kid-safe appliances

When shopping for appliances, consider durability, style, and, of course, safety features. For ovens and ranges, make sure that they have not only safety locks but also adequate thermal insulation to prevent burns from occurring, should anyone accidentally brush up against them. Stove knobs shouldn't turn too easily or should be placed on the back of the stove top, rather than up front and low where little hands can easily reach them.

Microwave ovens are incredibly convenient for modern lifestyles, drastically reducing cooking and clean-up time. But for children, they can be a serious hazard because of their user-friendly accessibility. Make sure your microwave oven is inaccessible to young children and has safety-programming features.

In checking out the design of any appliance, make sure that children won't hurt themselves on sharp edges or be able to accidentally open something while leaning against it. Refrigerators should be especially difficult for toddlers to open. Cords should be hidden and out of reach, as well. Don't forget to cover all other visible outlets with plastic protectors.

Surfaces should be easy to clean. Although stainless steel looks fabulous, you'll have to work hard to keep fingerprints off. A slightly textured surface, like that used on many refrigerators, is a good alternative because it minimizes fingerprints, but it needs frequent cleaning to prevent it from looking grimy.

KITCHEN SAFETY

- Do a test run for safety when childproofing the kitchen; look at things from a child's perspective, and work from there.
- Set up a safety zone—that is, one where it's always OK for your child to stay.
- Place fragile items and dangerous appliances out of reach.
- Teach your child the rules of safety, but still remain vigilant.
- Check for safety features on all appliances and electrical equipment you buy.
- Style and design matter everywhere; once you've decided that something is safe, make sure it works with your decor.

OPPOSITE The look of appliances in a kitchen is as important to its appeal as any other detail. A gleaming, stainless-steel refrigerator and stove add glamour and provide a welcome contrast to the wood cabinets.

STYLE FILE: color palette

Kitchens can often benefit from a healthy dose of color. Whether you want bright, cheery walls or a muted, neutral background with a few colored appliances or pieces of furniture, any combination can work for your personal style and your family's needs. Adding some bright color gives your kitchen a friendly atmosphere. In compressed spaces, color can make a once-dull space interesting and lively.

Weathered or old furniture can be updated with a coat of shiny latex paint in fun colors like apple green, bright blue, or even stark white to contrast with colored accessories, and make the kitchen inviting to kids.

Color can be used creatively to evoke a particular atmosphere in the kitchen. Use your imagination to achieve the effect that you want, whether it's a fun hub of activity or a Zen-like sense of tranquillity. Color brings the look of a kitchen together, tying its practical functions together with its visual appeal. It underscores the notion that it is not only the working center of the house but also an informal welcoming space where the family gathers. Strong or bright tones can help blend in additional storage space or even make a compact space feel larger. If you don't paint the walls, small touches of color can also bring a distinct touch to a kitchen, whether it's one bright piece of furniture, like a table or countertop, or the addition of colorful accents throughout against a white or neutral-toned background. If you opt for a more muted look, subtle changes in tones can also give a kitchen a richer texture and make it more dramatic.

LEFT Paint cabinets in pastels, ranging from mint green to Pepto-Bismol pink for an off-beat but soft and inviting look in a kitchen short on space. In this one, lavender walls complete the playful aesthetic, while the kitchen table and chairs are kept in natural wood or neutral tones to keep from driving the look over the top, so people of all ages feel welcome.

OPPOSITE Add bright colors to make a room pop. These fuchsia-painted chairs pulled up to a table with a gingham table-cloth are set off against the whitewashed bead-board walls for a colorful yet fresh aesthetic in this kitchen's dining area.

COLOR PALETTE

- Choose your background color carefully. Whether you opt for a bright color or a neutral shade, keep in mind that the one you select may dictate the rest of the kitchen's decor.

- Avoid using flat paint in the kitchen; it won't wipe clean.

- If you have an open-plan kitchen, make sure the color goes well with the living room.

- If your kitchen has contrasting surfaces, be bold and make a statement with your color choice. Remember: These surfaces can balance the look of either a dramatic color or a stark white.

- To give the kitchen a special touch, add accents on the walls and especially in glassed-in cabinets. Consider decorative plates, beautiful stained glass, or whatever your whimsy.

- If you opt against lots of color with your paint choice, add splashes of it throughout with tablecloths, plates, and napkins.

- Don't forget window treatments. Beautiful solid fabrics or trendy toiles can add kick to any kitchen space. Of course, remember to keep the curtains away from any source of heat.

UTILITARIAN spaces

It's easy to overlook the spaces where the necessary minutiae of life take place: the entrance to the house, the place you hang your coat or place your keys, the hallway that stores hats and gloves, or the bathroom where you start your day each morning. Despite their small size, many of these spaces do affect your life. The mudroom, laundry space, bathroom, and other nooks and crannies that you don't often think about in the grand scheme of decorating are often areas where you spend lots of time without even realizing it. Think about the time it takes to get ready to go in the morning and ready for bed in the evening: If forty-five minutes daily doesn't seem like much, add it up. It's almost eight hours a week, thirty-two hours a month, and four-hundred hours a year! That's more than two weeks! And the mudroom is where the entire family enters and leaves the house every day. You may not spend long periods of time there, but as the last place you see before leaving your home and the first place you see upon returning, it assumes greater significance—and even ten minutes a day adds up quickly.

But before you drive yourself crazy with mathematical equations, think instead about how every little space in your home matters for you and for your kids. Even the most seemingly mundane space serves a utilitarian purpose. After all, a home should be enjoyed in every respect, and that means looking after all its respective parts.

The key to maximizing such spaces lies in the organization of each individual space. A highly efficient laundry room not only makes cleaning simpler, it may even make the chore of doing laundry more enjoyable. A mudroom that's a disorganized pile of mittens and soccer cleats can become an ordered storage haven, and a well-organized bathroom can only make your daily time there more pleasant, even for the kids. With organization, these spaces also become more user-friendly for them, too, especially places like mudrooms and hallways that they use often.

OPPOSITE Place a simple, wooden bench at the entrance of the house to serve as storage for rain gear and other assorted belongings. Paint the floor an interesting color, like this cheery yellow, to contrast with the gloom of rainy days.

function
meets style

But what truly transforms these spaces is a decorative makeover. A splash of color, wallpaper, or other painted details you don't want to indulge in the main rooms of the house can have full reign here. Because these spaces are out of sight from most guests, you have the chance to be a bit daring. Think of it as an experimental part of decorating the house. If an idea you're hesitant to use on a larger scale makes you too nervous to try elsewhere, give it a chance here. Funky shelving, feminine floral details, or bold chrome fixtures are all viable possibilities. And the utilitarian rooms of the house, no longer ignored or forgotten, will soon rival the rest of the house in their style and comfort for the whole family.

Giving order to a space while adding a touch of whimsy not only streamlines the way your family lives but also puts a smile on your face or bestows a few minutes of serenity as you enter or leave your house or as you do a daily chore. And you should never underestimate the importance of that.

LEFT Transform an entrance into a sometime mudroom. Even just a small closet, a rustic umbrella stand, and a wooden footstool can make the entryway useful as a mudroom. Lay down a doormat to keep from trekking in debris from the outside world.

mudroom

The classic mudroom probably proliferated first in New England. Northeasterners like their grand entrances as well as anyone else, but with the frequency of murky weather and with a mud season to contend with, a more casual side entrance as a place to store dirty footwear and winter layers must have emerged as an alternative to sullying the pristine main entrance and foyer. The rest of us caught on quickly, amending our side entrances even without the temperamental springs and winters of the Northeast.

But the first mudrooms of yore have quickly grown up into catchalls that both complete and organize a modern household. In the largest examples, the addition of hooks, tables, mail slots, and message centers have transformed mudrooms into sophisticated anterooms. And if your house doesn't come with one, be creative. If you can fit in a few hooks and attractive baskets or cubbies into the entrance hall, that space can easily transform into a transitional space where pet supplies, backpacks, schoolbooks, sporting equipment, and shoes can be accommodated.

Storage

Closets, closets, and more closets are the most helpful way to arrange a mudroom. Seasonal items that most likely won't be used as often—like ski equipment and tennis rackets—can be stored away on shelves, in boxes, or in other crannies. A row of pegs or hooks can help arrange coats or umbrellas. A small table for keys, mail, and other objects should be placed near the entrance. A shoe rack, umbrella stand, or hamper also helps matters during the wetter months.

RIGHT Add shelves, cubbyholes, and sliding wire baskets to help arrange belongings in the mudroom. Use the closet space to hang coats, and add a low bench to help the transition from muddy boots to clean house slippers.

Entrance Hall

Even if you don't have the luxury of a mudroom, entrance halls are still transitional spaces, and they can be encouraged to function as such. A closet or shelving will help streamline the daily detritus. Inexpensive, easy-to-clean flooring is a must. Opt for attractive doormats, washable area rugs, or a painted and sealed floor cloth. Or if possible, redo the flooring with water-sealed ceramic tiles; cleaning will never be easier. Shaker-style pegs or hooks are helpful too—especially if closet space is lacking. Cubbies or baskets for shoes help reduce the flow of dirt into the rest of the house.

ORGANIZING: family message center

If the key to easy, efficient living is staying organized, then there is nothing better than having a space in the home dedicated to just that in a message center. It's a miniature news kiosk where soccer games, business dinners, and PTA meetings get recorded so that everyone in the family is aware of family happenings, making communication simple so that nothing falls between the cracks.

LOCATION

An entry foyer or a corner of the kitchen may seem like the most logical place for a message center, but really it should be wherever makes sense for your family. Underneath a second-floor landing, in the living room, or on the wall of an office are all possibilities. Anywhere you can fit a board for posting messages and invitations or a calendar will work. Do put it in a central location, though, so that everyone in the family sees it regularly without having to make a special trip for it. With a little improvisation, you can make it an asset to your home rather than an eyesore. A French-style upholstered board that is quilted with ribbons offers an attractive way to integrate a message center into a room's decor. Daintily pretty, crisscrossed ribbons allow invitations, photos, and papers to be posted in its corners. A corkboard can be covered in any fabric of your choosing and surrounded with a painted wood frame. A magnetized surface such as the refrigerator works just as easily, though. Add an oversize calendar to keep a visible reminder of family appointments, and invest in some fun magnets.

HIGH-TECH COMMUNICATION

A corner of the office or den is also a spot where family messages and calendars can keep everyone up to speed. If spreadsheets and computer printouts are your primary mode of communication, the message board should be located where it is convenient to the computer. Just make sure that a board or a part of the wall surface is kept clear for posting messages in the open for everyone to see. And even if the message board is located in what is primarily a work space, family photos and artwork can still figure into the mix to keep things cheerful.

OPPOSITE Liven up a message board with bits of ribbon and colorful pictures. Bookshelves and boxes in this family work space store both office supplies and kids' art supplies. Spice up a message board with a fun design like this diamond-pattern board.

laundry room

In households with children, the stream of laundry to be done is never ending. But there's no reason why a working laundry room shouldn't be cheerful, too. First, for functionality, the laundry room should have several shelves and durable, waterproof surfaces. If you have a laundry-size sink at your disposal, a waterproof working space nearby for laying items flat before they're hung can come in handy. A place to stow baskets or a built-in laundry hamper minimizes the need to carry heavy loads of clothing, too. Add a stool or chair to the mix to allow a little break for daydreaming or for some company, especially for the children. Bright lights, a folding table, and a fold-out ironing board (which can also conserve valuable space) are other essentials. As in the kitchen, remember to keep detergent, bleach, and other potentially hazardous substances out of the reach of children. A high shelf or even a cabinet with a safety lock will suffice.

Decorative Touches

Touches like pretty framed prints, plants, and striped or brightly painted walls add cheer to your work space. Go from drab to daring with funky striped walls or interesting prints. If there's a space between the cabinets and the ceiling, don't neglect it! Potted plants or bright borders complete the overall effect. A framed print that doesn't fit in elsewhere in the house could be perfect here. A message board with reminders, lists, and pictures is a good way to prompt some thinking while you fold laundry. Add touches of whimsy by hanging vintage or antique laundry artifacts or signs. Flea markets, antique fairs, or yard sales are great places to scavenge for these. Even the tiniest odds and ends of rustic Americana can give your laundry room a lively, countrified look that is more appealing than white, sanitary, and dull. Vintage plaques, pieces of patchwork quilt, or wicker can also add interest to a laundry room, as can delicately feminine drawings and Victorian-style baskets hung on the walls.

LEFT Add interesting details to give an otherwise pure-white laundry room a bit of pizzazz. The hamper doors that resemble whitewashed shutters, bright prints, and an antique washing board propped against the wall enliven this room. Baskets and glass jars hold loose ends, whereas a simple bulletin board is perhaps the best accessory, holding family pictures and mementos.

OPPOSITE Down to the drain in the middle of the floor, this workroom is highly functional and completely waterproof, but the jazzy waves and portholes of the paint job keep it far from dreary utilitarianism.

kids' bathrooms

Like the laundry room, the bathroom shouldn't be thought of as purely functional. It's as important for kids to feel comfortable and at home here as in any other part of the house. Make the bathroom a pleasurable, comfortable place to be, and before you know it, your children will forget that washing up used to be a chore. Just as it's important for you to have relaxing downtime in the bath, it's equally important for kids!

Proportion and Size Considerations

The most common problem in kids' bathrooms is negotiating the proportions. Adult-size sinks, countertops, and cabinets are gigantic for a 4-year-old, just as something built for a 4-year-old is outgrown by the time the child turns 8 or 9. Try to find ways to make the bathroom accessible for everyone. This usually means adding a step stool, but it could also mean installing adjustable touches like hooks, towel racks, and handles at child-friendly heights, which can always be moved up later. Or, if you have room, a free-standing towel rack might be easier to add.

KID-FRIENDLY: waterproof surfaces

Messiness in a child's bathroom, a laundry room, or a mudroom is understandably a given. But making sure surfaces in those rooms are waterproof and safe is a must. Test out the surfaces of floors, bathtubs, and showers before children have a go in them. If the surfaces are slippery, add a rubber-backed or skid-resistant mat to catch little feet before they have a chance to skid.

Ceramic tiling on the floor, walls, and counters of a bathroom, mudroom, or laundry room is easy to clean, available in endless color options, and waterproof as long as the tiles are properly sealed. On floors, however, they may be slippery, so remember to add bath mats or nonskid, canvas coverings to ensure safety.

Although marble is a pricier option, it's also easy to maintain. Its slick, grainy appearance can lend a more serious air to a bathroom. Even in tiny doses—for example, on countertops or in the shower— marble gives a bathroom or any other space a timeless appeal.

In bathrooms, treated wood is an option for cabinetry, walls, and even counters, but it's probably best to reserve wooden floors for other parts of the house. Laminated plywood can be made over in lots of colors and is as water resistant as a tiled or marble surface for countertops. Wooden floors in a mudroom are acceptable and have a rustic appeal as long as they've been treated and floor coverings or entrance mats are in place so that feet can be wiped clean before entering.

Kids' Creativity for the Bedroom

Because kids' bathrooms are less visible than other rooms in the house, their decor can get creative and even a little funky. Be sure your children know that their opinions are always welcome, but make this especially so in rooms meant primarily for their use. Bright colors, painted designs, and colorful toys can be included in the bathroom area. Shower curtains and bath rugs are easy ways to brighten the space. You can even let your kids personalize their area by painting it themselves. A wall of colored handprints from their younger years could remain as nostalgic handmade wallpaper for years to come.

Organized Storage for a Small Space

As you create a welcoming space, storage and a functional layout are also important considerations in the bathroom. Because fun often goes hand-in-hand with messiness, a well-organized bathroom that's kid-friendly is a challenge to maintain, but it doesn't have to be impossible. Make sure you provide lots of shelves, cabinets, or baskets for organization. Hampers for dirty clothes and towels are a must. If your bathroom is short on space, try baskets underneath the sink or hung on the back of a door. For young children, having toys and waterproof books close at hand in the bath is key to making the bath an enjoyable experience. Install a storage space to hold all the bath accessories. A short plastic cart with pullout drawers does the trick if it can be placed next to the tub.

OPPOSITE Let your imagination go with a bright-and-bold mural. The outsize salamanders and turtles announce that this is a child's space, but they're sophisticated enough to appeal to adults, too. And with plenty of shelves for storing towels and other bathroom essentials, practicality isn't overlooked.

RIGHT Hang a woven laundry basket on the back of a bathroom door that needs to conserve valuable floor space. Wet towels and clothing will be ready for washing without cluttering the floor.

SHOPPING: fixtures and fittings

A bathroom's fixtures and fittings are important in creating the look that you want. From stainless steel to brass to nickel, everything from the bathroom's faucet to the towel racks will gleam with the metal finish you choose. Regardless of the material, however, it's probably best to keep a uniform look for all fittings. This will bring any other disparate materials together and help the bathroom look cohesive. For example, wooden cabinets, bright blue tiles, and a frosted glass shower may seem like an over-the-top combination, but with the same metal-toned fittings bringing it all together, the bathroom looks like a made-to-order dream.

METAL COLOR CHOICES

Depending on what look you want to achieve, silver- or gold-colored fixtures and fittings will make a difference. Brass and copper tones can give a warmer feeling to a bathroom, whereas stainless steel and nickel can project cool sophistication. If you can't decide between them, two-tone fittings will make the grade. Different metals range greatly in price, however, so beware. Stainless steel is generally much less expensive than similar-looking nickel, and gold-plated metals are lower on the price spectrum than brass or copper. But if you decide to keep costs on the low side, there's no need to sacrifice looks. Shop around. Many stores today offer complete lines of affordable fittings and fixtures in a variety of traditional and modern looks. If there's room in your budget for pricier options, look at top-of-the-line manufacturers such as Waterworks, Dornbracht, or British import Czech and Speake. Any of these are sure to meet your style needs and should be durable enough to serve the whole family for years.

STYLE AND CONSISTENCY

What style of fixture should you choose? A funkier, more modern look may be a fun choice in the children's bathroom, but a more traditional style would carry the bathroom through years of different paint jobs and adjusting tastes. As when picking finish colors, the best choice is to remain consistent throughout the bathroom. A futuristic-looking faucet may look strange with Federal-style molding or wainscoted walls. Similarly, super-slick fittings in a rustic, wood-outfitted bathroom would also seem out of place.

When winding down the home stretch of decorating the bathroom, or any room for that matter, it may seem like the best choice is the easiest, but consider the wealth of options out there before making a final decision. Just remember: In a small space like a bathroom, pulling together a stylish, kid-friendly space is all in the details.

OPPOSITE Place freshly washed towels at the ready for guests, and add touches like fresh flowers or sweet-smelling soaps to make anyone who uses the room—guest or family—feel at peace.

shared bathrooms

Things undoubtedly get a little more complicated when there is more than one person using a bathroom. In an ideal world, there would be a bathroom for each person in the house, but the reality is that sharing is unavoidable in most households. Sharing space in the bathroom can be difficult if you have an inquisitive 5-year-old and a cosmetic-happy teenager sharing storage space, or if you have a mix of teenage boys and girls who all want their privacy. The best solution is to design the bathroom to be versatile enough to suit many needs.

To begin, double sinks are a necessity. They'll double any bathroom's productivity by allowing for simultaneous teeth brushing and hair combing and can generally alleviate Monday-morning mayhem. If possible, each child should have his or her own set of drawers, storage space, and towel bar or hook to ensure that there's some sense of privacy. If there aren't enough drawers for that, try different-colored storage caddies stowed in a cabinet or on a shelf. A bathroom that connects between two children's rooms is a plus. Both have their own entrance and at least the illusion that the bathroom is their own.

LEFT Two of everything in this bathroom, down to the cubbyholes, lets kids divide space equally. By adding open storage space, you'll free up counter space, and still keep stored items visible. Let kids add their own touches, like the beanbag toys at the windowsill, to personalize their space.

OPPOSITE Pair chrome fittings with minimalist, sand-colored tiles and warm, brown paint for a sophisticated, contemporary look. This extra-large sink works well in a shared bathroom.

A Parents', Kids', and Guest Bathroom

If adults and children will be sharing a bathroom, it's important to make it comfortable for people of all ages. Toys can be kept to a minimum, along with any other bathroom clutter. Swap stuffed animals for framed prints for a more sophisticated look. Make sure the bathroom is as soothing and welcoming to children as it is to adults.

If a bathroom will double as a guest bathroom, make it especially user-friendly. Clean towels should be readily available as well as soaps and shampoos. Storage space remains important, but glass cabinets can be a more inviting choice, because they allow guests to feel that they're welcome to use anything in the bathroom and they won't feel like they are snooping.

No matter what the look or the purpose of your bathroom, make sure it's a comfortable space. From colorful and playful to white and serene, a bathroom should be as functional as it is attractive.

ABOVE One brilliant way to deal with multiple users is to create a separate room within the bathroom for the shower or bath. This shower room makes it possible for one person to shower while another uses the outer bathroom area. The cobalt blue wall helps define the shower as a separate space, enhancing a sense of privacy.

OPPOSITE If you pare down to your top priorities, storage can always be found for what is essential. This bedroom has largely been pared down to two essentials: storing an extensive record collection and providing a serene sleeping space. An old army chest adds a graphic touch and a bit of extra storage at the foot of the bed.

STYLE FILE: storage solutions

In any utilitarian space, storage is paramount, and finding attractive and colorful ways to store things is a prized ability. Drawers, boxes, and cubbyholes are musts, everywhere from the sparest of mudrooms to the most cluttered of bathrooms. In small rooms, maximizing the space you do have is essential. Stack boxes on shelves to store away extra papers and knickknacks. Cubbyholes or pullout shelves are another way to store items while keeping them easily accessible.

BOXES

Boxes are one way to store items that are used less frequently. Placed on shelves and in cabinets, they let you further organize your storage spaces and keep visual clutter to a minimum. In the bathroom, they can hold necessary but little-used medicines and first-aid equipment. In a laundry room, sewing equipment that should be kept out of reach of children finds the perfect home in a series of stacked boxes. If you want your children to have access to what has been stored in the boxes, put labels (or pictures) that they can read on the boxes. And, whether you like them in wood, striped cardboard, or painted galvanized metal, storage boxes can add another colorful touch to your decor.

CUBBYHOLES

Cubbyholes are another innovative way to expand storage in a shelving unit. Where once only a stack of towels or a few hats would fit, cubbyholes inserted into a space can increase storage tenfold. A mudroom benefits from superefficient cubbyholes that separate hats from gloves from scarves, so they're easy to find when you're rushing out the door. Likewise, in a bathroom, clean towels are ready to grab as soon as you step out of the shower.

THE IMPORTANCE OF BEING EFFICIENT

The tiny work spaces of a home are just as important to the entire family's well-being as any other part of the house. From mudrooms to entrance halls to laundry rooms, a stylish space that serves its needs is the epitome of a well-run household. And don't forget to love those parts of the house like any other. They're the cogs that make the rest of the house function well, and they deserve to be treated as such. Paying attention to style and function in these utilitarian rooms is a surefire way to help your home become what it needs to be for your family to enjoy it to the fullest extent possible.

OPPOSITE Place a small set of cubbyholes atop a desk to help organize supplies—in this case for sewing. The soft green paint blends with the wall and is the perfect foil for the bright colors of the thread and ribbon.

ROOM TO RETREAT

STUDIES AND STORAGE

CHILDREN NEED A RETREAT IN THE HOME, SAME AS YOU DO. Unless space is abundant, children often sleep, study, play, and store personal items in their bedrooms. This multipurpose approach is certainly doable, but to create an attractive, organized, child-friendly space with all these functions takes planning and research. Before making any purchase, think about how to make the room's design work hard. Your child should want to spend time in the room, enjoy it, and be comfortable doing homework and projects there.

For this book, I interviewed and observed children ages three to nine and was impressed with how much each loved his or her room and had definite ideas about what he or she liked and needed. While a three-year-old can not be interviewed per se, I spent time in many kids' rooms and noticed how they loved being there. From sunny rooms with great treetop views of the neighborhood, to rooms with plenty of floor space on which to spread games and toys, the best designs are rooms that can grow with the children.

This chapter includes children's bedrooms that accommodate various activities. It also describes situations where study areas are merged with family spaces. The latter examples illustrate how, if a bedroom is too small for a desk or storage, these functions can be successfully introduced in common areas. Whether you have to split your child's activities between rooms or not, it's worth the effort to create a retreat that gives them space—quiet space to read, think, imagine, and study.

Storage by Design

Storage space is critical to making bedrooms work and should not be overlooked in the plans for children's rooms, no matter what their age. Plan to devote a corner or part of a wall to book storage. In fact, the more places your child can access reading material, the better. Consider installing a single shelf right near the bed so your child can choose the evening's storybook and stuffed animal easily.

If your children's rooms are big enough for them to play in, consider having carpeting or a throw rug on one side and linoleum on the other—a wet and dry side. Kids can learn to bring out their paints on the wet side, and you don't have to warn them to be careful so often.

Toys, drawing materials, and prized homework all need an easily accessible storage place. Toys can go into all kinds of imaginative containers that can coordinate with the room's palette. For example, buy wicker laundry baskets and spray-paint them. Teach your children colors and names by painting them different colors and making signs for what's inside; use one for trucks, another for balls, etc.

Drawing materials can be kept in cardboard boxes that the children decorate to match the room. Boxes can be painted or accented with fabric swatches that match the curtains or borders you've chosen. This kind of activity stimulates creativity and gives children a sense of ownership and orderliness.

Above: Here is a creative, attractive way to make storage a major design component in your child's room. Open shelves with varying depths allow a mix of objects to be stored and offer opportunities to segregate and organize items. Cabinets keep frequently used toys in reach and can hold awkwardly shaped items.

Above: Another way to coordinate storage areas and save money is to purchase sturdy wooden furniture from a secondhand store or flea market and hand-paint it to match the theme of the room. Here, a desk and storage bin have been painted with a nature theme.

Storage as a Design Element

One thing every parent soon realizes is that there can never be too much storage space. With each growth phase come more books, drawing tools, toys, sports equipment, clothes, videos, CDs, and more. These things spill into the rest of the house if storage in the bedroom is inadequate. With a little creative planning, you can find storage solutions that not only are practical but also become a major design element in your child's room.

If budget allows, consider building in bookshelves and anchoring them with storage cabinets. The more space devoted to them, the better items can be stored and displayed. Two shelves assigned to colorful stuffed animals become a design element. Store items your children play with frequently on the lower shelves and cabinets. The cabinets can be used for their favorite items, and because they have doors that close, mess is not an issue. This system works well for children of all ages. Young children, in particular, like to go into their own cubbyholes for their toys.

Another option, if your child will remain in this room for several years or if space is limited, is to work with a carpenter to custom-design a structure that accommodates storage and a work surface. A simple, clean-lined design in wood allows you to easily change the room's palette to accommodate the next child, girl or boy, and remains in style for several years.

If both space and budget are limited, consider having a single custom-built piece that, by it's design, gives your child's room a dash of color and whimsy. It may function at first as a toy and book storage area;

Above: Utilize wasted space by building a window seat with storage underneath. Here, adding a Humpty Dumpty hat rack introduces color and texture to a wall while adding more practical storage.

Opposite: If you have the space to put a window seat along a wall, obtain even more storage by putting drawers beneath. In this room, the window seat is wide enough for a few children to sit and read, with easy access to books and toys below.

later, when your child is older, it may be better suited for clothes or sports items.

See whether or not the windows can accommodate a window seat. This is a great way to utilize what could be wasted space and to offer your child a pleasant place to read or play—with storage beneath. A window seat can be custom built, or you can improvise with a big, flat-topped trunk or toy chest. If the trunk needs sprucing up, tackle the painting project together with your child.

Another terrific storage solution is an armoire. Depending on your preference, choose an antique, a family heirloom or hand-me-down, one that's unfinished (ready to paint), or a flea market find. The latter two can be painted to match the room, or have some fun and paint on a pattern, texture, or outdoor scenes. A carpenter can add shelves, if necessary, and leave the bottom like an open bin for even more storage.

Personalizing the Study Zone

Children's study areas, perhaps more than any other area in their rooms, reflect who they are, what their interests are, and who they are becoming. They come here for privacy, inspiration, reflection, and creativity. When it's time to decide where to put the desk—in front of a window or tucked into a corner—ask them where they would like to be. Plan the study area with your son or daughter, with you guiding the discussion and inviting feedback. The goal is to create a place to which your child feels connected and that you think works functionally and visually.

Where does planning begin? A good first step, after determining where the desk will go, is to ask your children for decoration preferences. Cue them to help. Your son, for example, may have tucked away his collection of dinosaurs but still likes looking at them. Suggest a shelf for them. The bright colors and varied shapes will provide texture and color in the space.

Other items that can enhance a study area are photos of family and friends, trophies, and framed school papers they are proud of. To ensure the area remains visually pleasing, provide the tools needed to keep these items organized. Here are some examples:

- Install bulletin boards—one for special school papers, another for drawings, and another for special dates like sporting events and recitals.
- Go to a flea market and look for unusual boxes in paper or wood, then create a collage on a shelf or the floor. If your daughter loves hats, for example, search for old hatboxes and create a windowsill display/storage area.
- Purchase new or old tin containers—the more variety in shape and size, the better. If they need to be freshened with paint, make this a joint decorating project with your child. Paint on letters that describe what will be stored inside, or just have fun and make bright, energizing design elements.
- Use curtains that have little pockets sewn onto them for storing light items like tiny toys, marbles, or even photos. Try making them yourself, using different materials for the pockets. Trim with ribbon, denim, or whatever suits your fancy.

Above and Opposite: These rooms offer well-lit study space and lots of places to personalize and tuck away treasures—desk, bookshelves, and a high shelf on the wall for display.

Above: Here is a great way to combine functions in a room. A floor-to-ceiling bookshelf acts as a room divider separating the study zone from the play area. Homework and drawings on the walls personalize the room.

- Purchase a variety of cardboard boxes and paint them with your child, or cover them in fabric that matches the room. Cut off the top closures and line the boxes up on the floor or a bookshelf.

- Find a three-panel privacy screen or room divider, cover it in fabric that complements the room, and stitch on a dozen pockets in different colors and sizes. Mix and match fabrics and patterns to make this even more visually appealing.

- If wicker is compatible with the room design, purchase a wicker hamper for toy storage. Spray-paint it to match the room, and line it with fabric that matches the window treatments.

- For big, awkward items, consider introducing a trunk for storage.

- Stackable plastic crates make a good, inexpensive storage solution. Remember not to put heavy, sharp objects in these, and don't stack them too high, just in case they tip over.

- If space is very tight and the window has an unattractive view, look into having a 2- or 3-foot-high (.6 m or .9 m) shelf made that sits on the windowsill and mimics panes. Do not do this, however, if the window functions as a fire escape.

Above: Take an inventory of your child's personal items and decide what you need to accommodate. In this room, the bunk bed had a desk and storage built in, but more freestanding storage was needed to accommodate games.

Left: If you're handy with a saw, cut plywood in an interesting shape to enclose your child's bed, then paint it to match a theme. For more storage, replicate the shape in smaller versions and close it with a roof.

KIDS' STORAGE IN **FAMILY LIVING SPACES**

Consider locating children's books and toys in family living space—try cabinets, bookshelves, even fireplace mantels. Thus, when you are in the kitchen or family room, you can converse with your children while they play or color. This is a wonderful way to show that children are on board, and it makes them feel as important as you in the home.

Take the same approach in bathrooms. Keep children's towels, soaps, and bath toys in lower cabinets or shelves so they can help prepare for their bath. Choose a small hamper for them to throw their own towels and dirty clothes into; it's a nice training ground for being orderly and responsible.

If you have pets your children can safely feed, consider storing the pet food in a place the children can access. Feeding pets gives kids a sense of ownership. Your child can paint or color a food holder for your pet hamster, bunny, or fish.

Set aside cabinet space in the living room or family room for children's toys. Children can go into their own cupboards and play while Mom or Dad is within range to watch them and chat.

Do you cook a lot? Put baskets of toys in lower kitchen cupboards. The children can play on the floor nearby while you work. Likewise, devote a low shelf in the kitchen or living room to toys or dry snacks so your child feels part of the family scene.

SOLVING THE **NO-CLOSETS** PROBLEM

The list of things you have to store for your children can send you reeling! Instead of panicking or threatening to throw out everything without a home, turn the tables and have a little fun. Here are some imaginative storage solutions to consider if you have a playroom but not enough closets.

Save old milk cartons, shipping cartons, and juice bottles. When they dry out, paint them and fill them with marbles, crayons, paintbrushes, rulers, and scissors.

Scour flea markets for old wooden boxes, or take apart an old desk and use the drawers as storage space; chances are they'll stack. Have the handyman of the house attach wheels to the boxes and drawers. Attach string or ribbon to the knobs and your children can transport drawers full of toys to the family room and back to their rooms in a flash. Decorate all of these with paint, fabric, or both.

Purchase a set of brightly colored bed sheets, feed a wire through the sewn ends, and attach the wire at ceiling height to two nails, one on each end. Or, purchase fabric and iron-on hems, and attach the same way to the wall. This wall of fabric will hide lots of toys.

Purchase a card table or two and cover with fabric; store toys and games underneath.

COMPUTER PLACEMENT AND STORAGE

It's best to put your child's computer in a public area of the home, according to *Boston Globe* parenting columnist and author Barbara Meltz, who researches children's computer usage *(Put Yourself in Their Shoes, Understanding How Your Children See the World)*. She urges parents to be involved in their children's computer activities. Show them that the computer is a useful appliance, not a form of entertainment. Monitoring is difficult if the computer is in the child's room, but if there is no choice, keep the modem in view so you can monitor Internet use.

Make sure the space accommodates the computer! Monitors take up lots of surface. Buy the computer first, then furniture. Install window treatments that reduce glare on the screen. Include your child in selecting the mouse pad. Myriad design themes are available, from cartoon characters to your own dog.

A chair that swivels and moves up and down is handy—the swivel for turning from the computer to another work surface, the height adjustment when children share the space.

Accent the desk with your child's prized collections. This work space should be both comfortable and inspiring.

Spend time with your child choosing a screen saver. Sound effects and action can enliven the space but may send the wrong message.

Choose sturdy desktop storage bins for supplies. Vary the sizes, shapes, and colors for visual interest.

Select a lamp that serves all the tasks undertaken at the desktop. Three-way bulbs offer both general and task-specific lighting. Floor lamps with adjustable necks illuminate both reading chairs and the computer table.

For instant neatness, house the computer in an armoire. New models are designed with computers in mind and offer storage as well. Antique armoires can be reworked for this purpose.

BATHROOM **TILES**

Today, bathrooms are given more and more design attention. If you step into a tile showroom these days, you will find a plethora of tiles specifically designed for children's baths and featuring themes from romping bears to Noah's ark. If you are considering devoting a bathroom in your home to a child or children, keep in mind these design guidelines and suggestions for tile use.

Consider using tile with geometric patterns or generic themes like the beach or animals if the bathroom will be shared by boys and girls.

For a boy's or girl's bathroom, consider border tiles that reflect their general interests, such as sports. Borders are easiest to change if your tastes change later.

Be careful not to choose trendy tile themes that may go out of style quickly.

Trail decorative tiles around a window frame, or make patterns on the floor. You can create interesting, amusing patterns that direct your child's attention to the sink, tub, shower, or a great view outside.

Accessorize with towels, towel racks, soap dispensers or soap dishes, wastebaskets, rugs, and wall hangings.

Anna's second drawing depicts a current favorite item in her room, her calendar. This can cue a numbers and time theme in which to redecorate.

- Allow Anna to draw an oversized monthly calendar on a roll of paper installed at her height on the wall.

- Cut out felt numbers, punch holes on the tops, string ribbon through, and hang with tiny nails or hooks across a wall.

- Zone the room by season. Paper each wall with an appropriate visual. Accessorize with stuffed animals that live in cold and warm weather, curtains with a sky or cloud pattern, or a miniature collection of sleighs on a shelf. Anna could draw snowflakes and hang them in the winter windows, and draw flowers for spring windows.

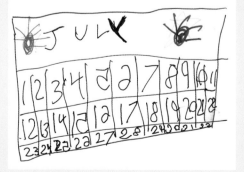

Anna

Anna's computer is in the family room. Asked if she could change anything in her bedroom, she drew a desk with a computer. Notice the attention to detail—two vases of flowers, a colored monitor, and desk drawer details. This six-year-old has a design vision!

However, Anna shares the computer with several siblings. Perhaps her parents can add a fresh-picked flower in a bud vase or a little plant that can be taken off the work surface for watering. It seems being pretty matters to Anna! Another way to personalize the computer area is to have photos of family members on a bulletin board nearby to generate a sense of community.

Miles

I think Miles really drew his life wish rather than what he wanted in his room. When I sat with him weeks before he drew this, he told me that he wished for a secret kitchen over his bedroom. That way, whenever he wanted a snack, he could climb into his secret kitchen and get whatever he wanted.

Actually, having a little box in his room, perhaps decorated with his drawings of food, could be a cute storage area for healthy snacks. It could hold a few small bags. That way, when he is playing by himself or with a friend, he can go to his own cupboard! An empty oatmeal box could become an art project to then store animal crackers or pretzels.

Miles is five and crazy about dogs. When I asked him what he wished he had in his room, he drew a dog at his computer! In reality, his computer is in his den, surrounded with plastic prehistoric animals.

The fact is, the timing is not right for Miles to have a dog—but he is taken with them. Perhaps a way to encourage his healthy appreciation of dogs is to bring a modest dog design theme into his room.

- Place a scatter rug with a big dog face at his bedside.

- Line a wall with a row of photos or drawings of his favorite dogs in the neighborhood.

- Find a dog clock that barks a different bark to mark each hour. Each hour has the face of a different dog. Alternatively, someone who is handy could make a clock with a dog's face.

185

AT MILES'S HOUSE

When Suzi and Steve bought a two-bedroom city condominium, they wanted to maximize their limited space and create a child-friendly, stimulating home for their son. One of the first things they decided to do was give Miles the bigger of the two bedrooms, the one with a pleasant bay window with city views. The goal was to give him a room where he could play, store lots of toys, and have a friend sleep over. Likewise, the second full bath was assigned to Miles and decorated for him as well. Responsibility for this chunk of real estate gives him a clear message that he is both important and accountable for keeping his things in order.

The large bedroom accommodates big, awkward items like a drum set and easel. If your home has similar space limitations, consider giving your child or children the larger bedrooms, assuming this makes sense given the overall layout. Suzi and Steve could have put Miles in a smaller room or even the den, which is in another wing. Sensibly, however, they realized that while he could bang his drums all he wanted there, storage would be inadequate. Containing bedrooms in the back wing and placing the living room, dining room, kitchen, and den in the front provide everyone with space for privacy and quiet when needed.

The fact is, Miles can play the drums in his room without bothering his parents in the front wing. If he challenges Steve to a game of chess, they can play in the living room or dining room.

Miles's board games, dinosaur collection, and computer programs are neatly arranged in the den. This room is nicely divided for Miles's games and his parents' books and equipment. He shares the computer with his dad, so Steve's work notes may be anchored by a convenient dinosaur!

Decorating Kid's Rooms and Family-Friendly Spaces

Another inclusive gesture Suzi made was to purposefully store things at Miles's level, within easy reach. "Everything should be easy for Miles to find—that way he doesn't have to constantly ask me where things are. Also, this lets him feel independent because he has access to these things—he has the sense that the house is available to him—except when it comes to food!" his mom says.

Shelves, bookcases, and storage drawers in Miles's closet all come in handy, and what goes where is up to him. Suzi observes, "It's his agenda, his choices. He feels he can go deep with that, on his own terms. And for him, as an only child, it works—his imagination becomes easily engaged."

She and Miles also spend time together in the kitchen. He enjoys working by her side, using measuring cups and stirring pots. Implements he uses are stored within his reach.

"We're in 1,500 square feet of space, and we've made it so he has choices on where to be—the den, his bedroom, the dining room—and with what—his books, cards, marbles, Beanie Babies. He doesn't need permission to do these things, and it gives him a sense of purpose and accomplishment. It has afforded him an 'I can do' attitude and lets him know he does not need someone with him all the time," she adds.

Opaque broad point pens:
red, blue, green, yellow,
white, and black

Two clear acrylic tool boxes
or organizer carry-alls

Crafter's glue
(make sure it adheres to plastic)

CRAFTING WITH KIDS

FUNKY TOOL BOX

Special boxes for special "tools" help keep things neat, and the boxes themselves can be lively additions to a child's space. Transform an ordinary tool box into a fun, personalized carry-all with easy to use paint markers. Kids of all ages can get involved—simply draw decorations on the clear box and use it to hold crafts, toys, school supplies, even as a lunch box. Paint marker ink takes a minute to dry, but once it does, it's permanent. This is a project for everyone in the family! Materials make two tool boxes.

INSTRUCTIONS

1. Plan your design. Make stencils by tracing the clipart below.

2. Shake and start markers according to package directions.

3. Beginning at the bottom of the box, place the stencils and trace around them, and color in the outlines. Or, if you are comfortable, decorate with free-hand shapes, numbers, and letters. To avoid smudges, allow each section to dry for one minute before you continue.

4. With crafters' glue apply buttons, small plastic trinkets, foam cutouts, feathers, or other found objects for a 3-D design. (Avoid using glitter—though fun and decorative, it tends to fall off. You'll be sweeping up glitter for months!)

5. The paint will dry in one minute. See manufacturer's instructions for glue drying time. Use your imagination and have fun.

TIP

Draw your words and pictures on plain white paper and tape them underneath the area you want to decorate. Then trace the designs with the color markers.

Photocopy at varying sizes

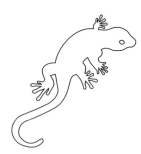

MATERIALS

Cork sheet 24" x 48"
(61 cm x 122 cm)

Ruler

Craft knife

White craft glue

Small paint brush

Acrylic paints, green
and dark green

Scissors

Modeling clay: black, red, turquoise,
white, yellow, and violet

Waxed paper for work surface

Clay blade or single edge
razor blade

Glass baking dish

Thumb tacks

FUN BUG TACKS AND
PAINTED CORKBOARD

Use your imagination to create fantasy clay bug thumbtacks that live on a painted grass cork sheet. Get kids involved in this project and have fun! The board will provide a special spot for your child's choice of art projects, school notices, or special photos to display.

INSTRUCTIONS

1. Roll out and flatten the sheet of cork. Measure, mark and cut three 6" x 24" (15 cm x 61 cm) strips of cork. Glue the 3 strips one on top of the other with white craft glue to create a triple thickness of the cork. Lay flat and let the glue dry.

2. Roughly sketch simple, grass shapes along the length of the cork. Paint them in dark green, and let dry. Sketch some more simple, grass shapes along the length of the cork, overlapping the darker, green shapes. Paint them in green, and allow to dry.

3. Create bug bodies from basic shapes. Roll the clay into balls of various colors and sizes from .25" (.5 cm) round to 1" (3 cm) round. Slice the balls in half with the razor blade. Make oval shapes and cut in half lengthwise. Roll out some flat sheets and cut wing shapes, small squares, and triangles with the craft knife. Dots can be made by rolling very small balls, and then flattening them out with your finger. Combine shapes to make the bugs. Make sure all colors and shapes are pressed together well before baking. Use a pencil point to make indentations for eyes.

4. Bake the modeling clay bugs according to package directions in a glass baking dish.

5. Glue thumb tacks to the backs of the bugs. Allow glue to dry. Hang the bulletin board to your wall using small nails or double sided tape.

TIPS

• Use a few heavy books to flatten the cork as the glue dries.

• Make extra bugs, and glue magnets on the backs for the refrigerator.

• Short Cut: Buy a decorated bulletin board so you can use your limited craft time on creature creation.

QUIET time

At times, everyone needs a quiet refuge in which to get things done. Adults need space to do paperwork brought from the office, to pay bills, and to write letters. Children need space to do homework, often on a computer. With more and more people working from home and with the increasing dependence on computers, which must find a home somewhere, the home office has evolved into a necessity rather than a luxury. Creating a welcoming home without areas that are off-limits is important, but having a quiet and comfortable office or study to which you retreat for private time or a chance to organize matters of the home or career helps keep your home harmonious.

OPPOSITE A small desk in a corner may be all the home-office space you need. Place attractive containers on the desk and a useful bracket shelf above to maximize storage. The pale green walls are serene, whereas the bright-blue desk energizes the space.

your "quiet time" needs

A requirement of the office or study is that it enable concentration, especially for taking phone calls and other business activities if you work at home. An enclosed space is highly desirable. Even if the area is tiny, the essentials—a desk, a chair, a computer, bookshelves, and some file storage—can fit in a space the size of a small closet. But if you can't have a room all your own, try sectioning off a larger room with a partition or some other type of divider that gives you the feeling of privacy. Think, too, about the type of work you'll be doing. Are you a freelance writer who needs lots of room for manuscripts and brainstorming? Make the space or room bright and airy, and maybe add a large desk and several bookshelves. Or, do you run a business that requires constant communication? Get plenty of file cabinets and storage space for your documents, and reserve areas for your fax machine, computer, and other necessities. Or perhaps the office is primarily used for paying bills and organizing the household. Will a file drawer and cubby slots be helpful? Will your children be free to use the office for homework or computer games? Specially designated storage space for their things can reduce clutter. Whatever your situation, the home office should conform to your needs, and the more you plan in advance, the more likely you are to adequately meet those needs.

Consider the Work Environment

Think about what surroundings help you to concentrate, particularly when it comes to color. Pick a soothing hue for your work space. A sterile environment never fosters creativity. Channel the things that make you feel peaceful, and translate them into the room. Are you enamored of nature? Fill the room with plants, and hang botanical prints on the walls. Does the ocean have a tranquilizing effect? Paint the walls a frothy sea blue, and furnish it with seashells and other nautical accents. Use your creativity. If blocky furniture isn't your taste, substitute a comfortable upholstered chair. Use an armoire to store your computer so it can be locked out of sight if you don't like its look. But most important, make your home office feel like a little haven where time to yourself can be both productive and calming.

TOP Use the same fabric all over, like the gingham check that hangs at the windows, covers the cushions, and is stretched across the floor in this room. It unifies a room with more than one function. A desk with a pullout drawer and a daybed allow an easy transformation from work area to bedroom.

ABOVE Hang artwork or decorations symmetrically on the walls to make a statement. Here, antique arrowheads are placed on parchment-paper backgrounds to offer inspiration to those who work in this space. Pair neutral tones with a bright background, like this yellow, for a maximum effect.

OPPOSITE Bright accents against white walls create a soothing feel in an artist's studio. Artwork and decorative accents above the mantel keep it from being an eyesore. Stow paints in corner when not in use, and use a dining table for a work space.

SHOPPING: desks and bookcases

From corporate-style desk units to painted wooden bookshelves to stainless-steel grid shelving, there are millions of furniture choices to outfit your home office. Consider the size, comfort, and functional aspects before buying. Look for drawers and shelves on a desk, but also note its height to make sure you won't strain your back while working. Ample surface area that fits the necessary equipment, from the computer to the fax to a desktop lamp, is also necessary. Make sure that you don't feel cramped and that there's plenty of room for you to work.

DESK STYLES AND MATERIALS

Desk units built expressly to accommodate desktop computers are another option. Armoires with a pull-down work surface or even the simplest Parsons table can be outfitted with the necessary accoutrements to give a desk a custom-made vibe. Some even have pullout drawers for keyboards that can be attached to the desk, as well as other convenient details.

Materials for desk units also run the gamut. A classic, wooden secretary desk looks elegant and hides clutter easily, but it has less work space; stainless-steel surfaces accessorized with funky, bright colors can alter the look of a room completely. Furniture you already own or find at a secondhand store can be refurbished. Paint wood a different color to match the rest of the furniture, or refinish an antique desk in a dark shade for more sober tones. If you're buying a new desk, examine it for durability. Do drawers roll smoothly? Will they still operate well when they're full of heavy paper?

BOOKSHELVES

Bookshelves and storage units are other major pieces you'll want to dwell on. A study with lots of book space can make for a striking effect. Take stock of your floor space and the size of your book collection before buying. Note the dimensions of the shelves to ensure that they can hold all your books, and that you can double-load if necessary. If you have a lot of oversize books, look for adjustable shelves. Make sure bookcases don't overpower the room. If you're feeling hesitant about covering the room in books, try shorter shelves that can be stacked higher if needed. Lacking floor space? Then try bracket shelves or recessed bookcases that won't intrude on the rest of the room, or alternate a stack of books with details like potted plants and photographs. If you have small children, all tall bookshelves or storage units should be fastened to the wall so they won't topple.

OPPOSITE Make your desk a statement piece by painting it blueberry blue like this scallop-trim desk from Maine Cottage, a furniture company. Little details can give a piece of furniture a whole new attitude. Pair it with Maine Cottage's Boothbay chair in orange for more punch.

HINTS FOR THE HOME OFFICE

- Assess how much storage space you need, and buy accordingly.
- Bring a measuring tape—height, width, and depth are all important. And be sure to write down your measurements from home when you go shopping.
- Make sure the available surface area accommodates everything from computers to lamps to paperwork.
- Look for a pullout shelf for your computer keyboard to save on space.
- Use stackable bookcases for a growing library.
- Add bracket shelves to substitute for artwork in the library.
- Bring out the color—paint a wooden desk a sprightly shade, or stain it a rich, chocolate brown.

family home office

When you get down to the basics, work is still work, and it takes a conducive atmosphere to get it all done. A home office needs to be quiet and comfortable. Balance your work needs with details that make you feel at home, and allow the space to blend with the rest of the house's decor. Put a warm carpet under your desk, and add a throw to your office chair. You should always feel at ease. Artwork is always welcome, as are stylish storage units. Even computer manufacturers have gotten design savvy, from Apple's colorful Power Macs to wafer-thin laptops, proving that the home office can look good and still be a place to get the job done.

Comfortable furniture is a must. Test out different chairs to make sure they're good for your posture and won't strain your back or neck while you log long hours on the computer. Don't assume the furniture has to look corporate, either. It's your home. Furnish it as you like. An oversize antique leather chair is just as at home in the office as a modular desk. An adjustable office chair can be comfortable for users of every age and height. If you like the comfort of an office chair but can't bear the look, you could try rigging a slipcover. Don't forget to test out desk height. Straining to work at a low desk is just as uncomfortable as a blocky chair. Make sure comfort is a priority, and style will follow.

Get Organized

Getting organized is another priority. Streamline your office or study, and you'll accumulate less clutter. Look for desks with storage units attached if you have mountains of paperwork that needs to be organized. Rolling file cabinets are also useful and can be tucked underneath a simple table desk or stowed away in a closet when not in use. Bibliophiles must invest in bookcases. Paperwork in file boxes can also be stowed out of sight in cabinets. Bracket shelves hung on the wall also adds storage space for books. Add framed pictures and plants to beautify the entire room. Fabric-covered or painted boxes add a decorative touch and are a departure from boring office neutrals. If the room's walls already sport a standout color, all-white or black accents will complement it nicely.

LEFT Ergonomic office chairs like this one can translate from the boardroom to the home office easily, and your back will thank you. Combine office furniture with warm wooden cabinets, plants, and a stylish, marble-topped desk to avoid an excessively corporate look.

ORGANIZING: family documents

Important paperwork accumulates quickly—medical records, schoolwork, travel documents, and financial records—and it's a lot to organize. To keep tabs on your family, it's essential to get efficiently organized, especially as your children get older. Don't just throw it all together in an office drawer. If you do, you'll never find that immunization record when your child is ready to head off for camp next summer or that Little League application you've just realized is due tomorrow.

One way to get started is to keep binders or hanging files for every member of the family, as well as for different household matters. Finances should be kept separately from medical forms, and all should be clearly labeled. You may even want to color code binders to correspond to each member of the family. Then they, too, will know which set of documents pertains to them. Try to keep everything inside clearly labeled and in chronological order, as well as up-to-date. It only takes a few minutes to add the latest paperwork to its corresponding folder when it's processed. Otherwise, you may find yourself swamped with stacks of documents that eventually take a whole rainy afternoon to organize. You'll thank yourself later for organizing now. If there's room, reserve a shelf or a drawer for each member of the family, too.

If you'd like to keep some papers in a confidential spot, invest in a desk or armoire with a lock so that your important papers are out of sight when not in use. Perhaps a series of shuttered file cabinets will do the trick. A fireproof safe for the most important documents can be a good idea. It can be stowed deep in a closet, out of sight. How often do you need to look at the title to your house, anyway?

RX FOR FAMILY DOCUMENTS

- Separate paperwork into categories—for example, medical forms, financial records, and schoolwork.
- Use labeled binders for each family member.
- Make sure all paperwork is up-to-date and filed chronologically, to keep your documents efficiently organized.
- Don't wait for a rainy day to put paperwork in its place. File each document as it comes your way.
- File all documents concerning the entire family in a separate binder.
- Stow confidential papers safely out of sight in a locked armoire, desk, or file cabinet.
- Keep an oversize portfolio for each child's "artwork" to prevent it from piling up and to keep it safe.

KID-FRIENDLY: lighting

You'll want to be sure your children's eyes aren't strained by excessive glare or lighting that's too dim. During the day, natural sunlight is best, but at night make sure the office, or any room, has plenty of bright light. Try to minimize or eliminate large variations and shady corners. Having to make rapid adjustments from light to dark areas can strain one's eyesight. Make sure the area surrounding the computer is bright, too, to avoid glare from the screen.

Overhead lights are harsh and should be eliminated or rarely used, particularly if there's a newborn in the household. Try to let in as much natural daylight as possible, but at night, softer, diffused lighting is easier on the eyes and more soothing. Floor lamps with swivel heads can cast a light upward and illuminate the entire room or can point down for reading. Clip-on desk lamps and other smaller task lights are also convenient, and can be moved easily and attached to almost any surface. Use energy-saving bulbs with the appropriate wattage. If you're feeling festive, you can add white Christmas lights that cast a lovely soft glow. Battery-operated children's night-lights not only welcome kids into a room but also add a gentle spot of light.

Most importantly, lamps are electric devices, so safety precautions should be considered in a kid-friendly home. Avoid plastic or halogen lamps. Both can get very hot to the touch and may cause serious burns. Cover all wall sockets with safety plugs when not in use to eliminate temptation, and clip loose cords to the wall, too. Anything hanging is a potential hazard.

Choose your lighting with caution and keep the safety of your children in mind. Assess the entire room when thinking about how to achieve a bright room overall, without shady spots or dark corners. Check for wattage and power, too, and try to buy the most efficient bulbs available. With these rules in mind, your home will be light, bright, and safe for all members of the household, not just in the office but throughout the house, as well.

LIGHTING 101

- Cast bright lights everywhere for an optimal working environment that won't strain your eyes.
- Get rid of shady corners; every spot needs light!
- Rely on swivel and clip-on lamps for versatility and convenience.
- Install three-way bulbs to adjust a lamp's brightness.
- Keep safety in mind. Don't use ultra-hot halogen lamps or malleable plastic.
- Cover all open light sockets, and tape down or hide any loose cords.

OPPOSITE Placing an office desk against a wall creates the illusion of a partitioned space, especially with an entire wall devoted to shelving. Add a fluffy shag rug for comfort, as well as a pair of chairs and a low table for another work space.

study/library

If you don't work from home, and a desk in the bedroom or kitchen is sufficient for your household paperwork, but you'd still like a space for quiet reading and reflection, just omit the office furniture and turn your extra room into a study or library. If that notion conjures up only images of dark, oak-paneled walls that reek of cigar smoke, think again. The studies and libraries of today have shaken off their dowdy image and can be designed with bright walls and exciting color combinations. If you find the look of floor-to-ceiling wooden bookcases too heavy, paint your shelves white or swap them for glass for a lighter, more ethereal look. Leather-upholstered club chairs not your thing? Cover the seating with dainty stripes or a cheery flower print. A feminine touch will always imbue a room with style. A spacious and light library can easily be a book-filled haven.

Without a desk and office chair, without file cabinets or the electronic equipment that goes along with a home office, there's room to spare in a study that's used more for relaxation than for work. However, it's still important for furniture to be comfortable. Think roomy reading chairs and sofas, or even a cushioned window seat for lounging. And don't forget to add plenty of lighting if you'll be doing lots of reading and working in this room. Three-way bulbs let you adjust lighting to three different levels, which is ideal if you don't have overhead or track lighting. Soft rugs and plenty of cushions and throws add to the comfort level as well. When the throws aren't in use, simply fold them up and store them in a designated area on the bookshelf, along with the extra pillows.

ABOVE A chartreuse-green daybed, which doubles as a sofa and an extra sleeping area, gives the room a color injection in this citrus-toned study. A freestanding bookshelf in another strong color, like this lavender, contrasts nicely and holds books, magazines, and games.

OPPOSITE A touch of leather in the library doesn't necessarily overpower, but use it sparingly as with this 1940s club chair in dark green. Add cushions or throws to soften the overall look. Glass bookshelves will lighten a space while holding your tomes.

convertible spaces

Because the study or office may sometimes moon-light as a guest bedroom or entertaining area, give careful thought to the use of space when designing these double-duty rooms. An office that needs to include both a desk and a pullout sofa, and still manage to convey enough warmth to allow guests to feel comfortable poses a creative challenge. To make the study-cum-guest room feel like a real room and not like a cubicle where you've happened to add a sofa, pay close attention to the details to pull it all together.

Office to Guest Room

One trick is to cover all upholstered furniture in the room in the same fabric, to give a cohesive look to the space. Accents added throughout that project a homey feel are always a welcoming touch. So often rooms that have two purposes lack a distinct personality—and no one wants to sleep in a room that screams "work." Your guests will feel as if they never left their own office behind! Make sure papers and other work materials can be easily stowed away when out-of-towners show up at your door for a visit. Maybe that means storing work materials like pens and pencils in chic leather-wrapped holders that are both visually attractive and serious enough for an office instead of plastic cups. What type of container do you like to look at? Use your creativity. Even glass mason jars (inexpensive and easily found at yard sales) can add a funky touch. If the room has a closet or shelving, be sure to leave some empty space so that guests can hang or store their clothing. And soft carpeting adds comfort for both guests and those who are hard at work in the home office.

OPPOSITE A home office goes from sterile workspace to cozy anteroom with the addition of feminine floral wallpaper and a smattering of houseplants. A simple desk can easily be cleaned of paperwork so that guests can use it.

STYLE FILE: comfortable nooks

Ever notice how there's always one comfortable corner in a room that people gravitate to? Like anywhere else in the house, such a spot exists in the office or study, and perhaps it's more important here than anywhere else to create a retreat where you can relax for just a few minutes while hard at work. A comfortable armchair to curl up in or a cushioned window seat form the cozy nooks that make a good room a great one.

Consider turning an underused corner into a focal point and favorite lounging space with just a few changes. Add a comfortable, good-looking chair in an eye-catching fabric. Stripes, checks, and plaids will do the trick. Think about the details that add comfort. Include a footrest, a table you can place a drink on, and a lamp for reading. Have a few cushions and a soft blanket at hand, and add tailored curtains in a colorful, textured fabric to cut glare and bring a sense of privacy. It will make the space one you can daydream in for hours on end. A window seat with matching cushions and curtains can make an irresistible space, especially for younger children who love constructing forts. Hanging children's artwork on the walls make a space feel loving, cheerful, and inviting to the whole family. A small throw rug or carpet keeps feet warm and adds a cozy feeling. Or, pair a low table with a couple of chairs in a corner, away from the desk, for sitting with family members or for sitting by yourself in solitary reflection, in a slight change of environment.

CREATING A NOOK

- Comfortable furniture is a must! Invest in an oversize chair or a padded cushion.

- Add to the comfort level with cushions and throws in soft fabrics.

- Cheer up a corner with bright fabrics. Then cover the furniture, curtains, and other accessories with the same pattern.

- Don't neglect the walls. Artwork, photographs, or message boards are ideal in a nook.

- Convert an unused ledge into a window seat with a thick cushion for reading or daydreaming.

- Place a low table and chairs in a corner to add a spot to socialize or for informal work.

OPPOSITE *An oversize wing chair in a nook makes all the difference. Cover it in a fabric like this cheery plaid, and add touches like dried flowers and a flowered lampshade to beautify your space without cluttering the desk.*

ABOVE *Even a nearly bare room can be a comfortable space. A bright, sunny room with clean, hardwood floors lures household denizens as easily as the most cushioned and tailored window seat.*

Office to Party Central

Even if your home office is being used as an occasional entertaining space rather than a sometime sleeping area, the same decorating rules apply. Make sure there's plenty of storage for when the room is used as an entertainment space so you can whisk important and unsightly papers out of sight. File cabinets, armoires, and boxes should do the trick. If you must keep certain supplies or tools out in the open or hung on a wall, think of them as artwork: Arrange them in the most aesthetically pleasing way possible. You'll be surprised how pretty your everyday objects can look. Pencils stored in miniature aluminum cans or world maps hung on the wall can create a stylish backdrop. But it's still important to personalize. A photograph or beautiful, small sculpture always has an appeal in a room, and you can intersperse such things with pencil jars and other utilitarian objects for a truly artful look. Look for objects like design-friendly metal wastebaskets and other office accessories that don't compromise style.

OPPOSITE Clear the usual clutter off a console table in the office to use it as a bar or buffet table for entertaining. Plenty of seating and a versatile table can serve dual purposes equally well.

PRIVATE spaces

Beautiful boudoirs don't have to be the pristine rooms of yore. A perfect-looking bedroom in a home is an antiquated notion. Children should be welcome in any room—including the parents' bedroom. Unfussy and comfortable master bedrooms, as well as comfort in the kids' rooms, should reign in a household. Think large, comfortable beds, simple linens, and soft flooring. Let the master bedroom's decor trickle down to the rest of the sleeping havens. For shared bedrooms (including those in vacation homes), an egalitarian attitude that's equally low-maintenance but still scores points in the style department shouldn't be forgotten.

OPPOSITE Soft, wall-to-wall carpeting and a big, luxurious bed make this serene bedroom inviting to all. The low height and lack of a footboard keeps the bed easy for everyone to climb into!

a room of one's own

Bedrooms are like sanctuaries. Everyone needs a private space to retreat to, whether you're heading to sleep or just for a brief time out. As your children get older and become more independent, their need for self-expression and private time emerges. Just like you, they need a space to call their own, where they'll be able to daydream, do homework, sleep peacefully, and have a bit of private time.

Children want to mark their own territory as their personalities become increasingly pronounced. Look inside any 13-year-old's school locker, and you'll find a plethora of snapshots, magazine clippings, sports paraphernalia, and drawings. Kids need to express themselves as their personalities are defined and sharpened, and what better place to do that than their own bedrooms? Try to be lenient with the decoration, and let your child's opinion and taste drive the decisions. They'll feel validated if you take their point of view seriously.

LEFT Although this master bedroom certainly looks grown-up, the cheerful, checked duvet cover, the bright, airy space, and the collection of miniature chairs along the top of the headboard make it an appealing space for children, as well.

A Kid-friendly Master Bedroom

The master bedroom is the domain of the adults of the house, but unless you're vigilant about keeping children out, there will be times, especially when they're small, when it feels like the family bedroom. Enjoy it; they'll be grown and gone before you know it. If you want your children to feel welcome and comfortable in your bedroom, it's easy to choose bedding and furnishings that are washable and sturdy. Keep extra pillows on the bed or close at hand so that you don't have to give up yours when they join you after a 3 A.M. nightmare. A comfortable armchair, especially one big enough for two, will see lots of use if you can fit it in.

Putting a few of their books on the bookshelf along with your own can both provide a distraction as you attempt to get dressed in the morning and makes an impromptu story time easy. Children love to look at photos of themselves "when they were little"—this is a good place to indulge in a few framed baby pictures. And delicate knickknacks and jewelry boxes are better kept on higher shelves or surfaces to keep them safe from inquisitive fingers. Your bedroom should be your peaceful sanctuary, but it will be all the richer for the happy memories created there.

ABOVE Managing to be both energizing and soothing at the same time, this pale-green master bedroom with chartreuse touches is very kid-friendly. Note the extra pillows, the fan placed well out of reach, and the steel and paper lamp that would probably survive being swept off the bedside table by an errant small foot.

ABOVE You don't have to forego flowers or decorative objects just because children will be passing through. Just keep them simple and largely unbreakable.

ORGANIZING: closets

Making method of a closet's madness shouldn't be such a daunting task. With a level-headed approach, the massive mountain of toys, mittens, sneakers, and clothes that come together in a jumbled mess can be organized into a well-ordered closet space. It's important to teach children at a young age that cleaning up after themselves and organizing their space is invaluable. Their own closets should make this easy by being kid-friendly and easy to navigate. Try not to have out-of-reach shelves or piled-high stacks of boxes. Hang clothing on low, easy-to-reach racks. If needed, a step stool encourages kids to reach for their things on their own.

Add shelves, racks, and hooks at all levels. Several companies make inexpensive closet add-ons, or you can check your neighborhood hardware store. Remember that children's clothing is smaller, so a rack that would have an adult-size suit dragging on the floor can happily hold a young child's clothes with room to spare. Shoe racks on the floor can hold several pairs, and a hanging version frees up valuable floor space. Shelves can hold cubbyholes for hats, gloves, belts, and other accessories. Hooks for coats or anything else should be low on the walls so that your child can easily reach them.

If a closet needs to hold toys, sporting equipment, and other items that can't be stored elsewhere in the room, get some stackable plastic boxes and label them so kids can identify what they're looking for right away, instead of digging through pile after pile. Try to place the boxes in a corner or out of the way of clothing and objects that need to be easy to get to every day. Resist the urge to place heavy or bulky items on high shelves, because they may topple over unexpectedly. Use wood, plastic, or fabric-covered hangers for kids instead of sharp wire. Look for hangers with clips for pants or skirts to hang clothes instead of folding them.

Once your child's closet is outfitted with all its shelving and storage needs, think about adding fun details or exciting colors. Paint the background in a bright yellow that complements the shades in the bedroom, to make your child smile every time the closet doors are opened. Borders that run along the top edge of the closet's walls also give a closet a whimsical touch. Kids may even stop thinking that straightening up the closet is such a drag.

OPPOSITE Closeted doors shouldn't mean forgoing style within. Add artwork like these sweetly feminine drawings, photographs, or a painted border to the wardrobe's interior. Notice the easy-to-reach height of the rack.

personal touches

A room that grows with your children and changes with their maturing personalities can be difficult to achieve while maintaining a budget. And a teen whose rapidly changing whims switch from loving pink one day to insisting on all black the next can't always be accommodated. Try to start with a few classic pieces that you both won't tire of quickly. A sleigh bed, a streamlined wooden vanity, or even an antique needlepoint rug can become a bedroom's core piece. Even family antiques can have a place in a child's bedroom and still last through the years. The heirloom cradle that your child quickly outgrew can become a favorite storage bin for stuffed animals. Bedding, curtain fabrics, area rugs, chairs, and wall hangings are easy to switch and can drastically alter the feel of a room.

A little self-expression is a good thing when it comes to your children's bedroom. Present them with choices so that they'll have ownership of their room. You can even let them have a go at decorating, within reason. Give them a vote in color schemes, fabric patterns, and furniture. Let your children express themselves in the details, and don't be afraid to let them have a little fun. Whimsical wallpaper and prints can fly in a child's bedroom where they wouldn't in the rest of the house. Let imagination run a little wild.

Wall Coverings

Start with the backdrop. The choices for wall coverings are endless, from simple, solid pastel paints to two-toned stripes to lively patterned wallpaper. If you pick something other than a solid color, make sure it can easily be altered if you or your child tire of its look. Hand-painted murals or patterned walls, for example, are difficult to paint over, and require several coats of thick paint. Wallpaper, although slightly more time-consuming to apply (you may want to hire a professional), can be stripped off and recovered. Try to stick to flat surfaces—grass or raffia walls may be fashionable and stylish, but they'll work better in a living room than a child's room.

Floor Coverings

Floor coverings should be given plenty of attention, as well. They can be painted, left untouched, or covered with carpeting. Although hardwood floors are beautiful and easy to maintain throughout the rest of the house, bare wood floors aren't very comfortable in a bedroom. Much play takes place on a child's bedroom floor, and slippery and hard surfaces can become a danger zone for younger children. Soft area rugs that are stain resistant or easily cleaned are a good choice. Pastel dhurries and rag rugs can work well with softer color schemes, and a bound carpet in a bold color can add a jolt of bright color and be a great place to flop for play.

Bed Coverings

Details are often what make a room unique and truly give your children a chance for self-expression. Their bedding is something that's as personal as the clothing they wear—and it's easy to give them the final choice. Fun designs for children's sheets have proliferated. In fact, many companies have bedding collections intended especially for children. Try department stores or mass retailers. You can never go wrong with classic monogrammed sheets, either. Most department stores will emblazon initials onto bedding for little cost, as will myriad catalog companies.

For matching details, look for fabrics that complement each other. Curtains and cushions don't have to be a perfect match, and they can always be replaced if the decor changes. Look for ways to let your children contribute their creativity. They can make a set of fabric- or paint-covered boxes in whatever shade they want. (This can be the place to let them include their latest favorite logos or characters.) Or let them have a bulletin board or art wall of their own design where they can pin things up to their heart's desire. That way, they'll always feel like their room is their own.

LEFT Your kids are sure to love these statement-making Marimekko bright stripes and bold flower prints splashed across their room. The Kukkaketo, Olkiraita, Silmu, Talvikki, and Seven Flowers patterns are shown here.

ABOVE A canopy daybed outfitted with hanging toys, puppets, or fabrics like this Anglo-Indian one is so inviting that bedtime will always be welcome. The canopy can always be dismantled if you tire of it.

COLORFUL escapes

Although it may have the most comfortably soigné of living rooms, the most flexible of studies, and the most welcoming of bedrooms, a family home gains immeasurably by containing another space that can take on many forms but is best described as a "colorful escape." This space may be a welcoming outdoor sitting area or a room dedicated to toys and games. It may be simply a family room where homework and crafts can be done, or an outdoor area where climbing structures and tire swings rule.

Whatever form it takes, it's a room where fun takes precedence, where you can shed your cares and enjoy family activities without having to accomplish anything. Whatever the uses of your family's play area, this chapter will help you make it a safe haven and outfit it to encourage your child's hobbies and passions.

ABOVE This colorful escape is a beautifully designed urban
backyard. Its structure is simple, but the reflecting pool at
one side adds intrigue, and the colorful, welcoming furniture
and the warm-red wall make the space feel alive. Don't be
afraid to use bright colors in outdoor spaces.

family playroom

In many homes, the room most fully dedicated to enjoyment is the children's playroom, but playrooms don't have to be reserved for just children; they can be used and enjoyed by the whole family. Everyone needs a space to let imagination flourish, and it helps if children, especially, have a domain where adult rules are more relaxed, where mess is tolerated (for a while), and where the physical-activity quotient can be higher. Decorate accordingly, and listen to your children's opinions even more attentively. Hang their artwork and projects on the wall; paint the room a bright, kid-friendly color; and add a whimsical detail that you know your children will enjoy. Above all, make sure it's a safe, comfortable area where children can entertain themselves for hours on end and develop their creativity to the utmost degree, without too much supervision or instruction.

Depending on your family's interests and hobbies, the play space can be used for any sort of activity. Make it a music room where the piano or other instruments are kept and played, or an arts-and-crafts center where children can paint and construct and where school projects can be completed. It can be simply a comfortable room where both children and adults can read, relax, play board games, or daydream. If you have teenagers, add a pool table or video games for a relaxing environment where they can stretch out, make some noise, and indulge their interests without disrupting activity elsewhere in the house. A small refrigerator stocked with cold drinks and snacks will further enhance the feeling that it's their own haven.

Converted basements, attics, unused garages (if you're lucky to have ample space), extra rooms adjoining children's bedrooms, or other little-used parts of the house are ideal for playrooms. If you're renovating by yourself, make sure that the room is properly insulated and that safety precautions are considered in your plans. Throw soft rugs on hardwood flooring for comfort if you forego wall-to-wall carpeting. Plenty of comfortable seating is important, too, and keep a large area of the room clear for playing. A low, child-size table is ideal for creating artwork and other creative projects. In warm climates, a part of the backyard lawn will work for a playtime space with a climbing structure, sandbox, and a table and chairs in an outdoor covered area. A play space should grow with your children, too: a playroom full of toy cars and dolls needs to translate into a lounging area with a television set and a couple of couches when your children approach adolescence or enter high school.

OPPOSITE Even if a space isn't solely dedicated to playing, fun touches like this sail fan, oversize fish lure, and surfboard bring to mind leisure activities and provide a reminder of escape from everyday life.

fantasy playroom

Let your children's playroom explode in a riot of color and whimsical details. It can go anywhere your imagination can take you. Do your daughters fancy a ladylike boudoir with books lining the shelves and dainty tables set for tea? Do it up in sweet pastels and soft fabrics. Cover walls and fabrics in pretty patterned wallpaper. But, instead of drowning the room in pink, add a contrasting shade like a mint green or citrus orange for a refreshing alternative. A pattern in small doses can keep things lively—think trim on the molding, carpet, or shades. It gives the room the ultimate ladylike touch for girls who love all things frilled and feminine. Or maybe you have boys who would like their own Amazonian rainforest to romp in. Paint your walls the lush greens and earthy browns of a wild jungle. Add a border of wild animals, or stencil vines on the walls. Make sure to include a space where the boys can build forts or roughhouse. Provide your children with spaces where their imaginations can run wild.

Stencil delicate detailing onto molding for a playful touch. What about a storybook fantasia setting? Cover the walls with scenes from favorite fairy tales and vine details throughout. More so than any other room in the house, the playroom is entirely the children's domain.

Color can add a friendly touch anywhere. Don't be afraid to go big, bold, and bright. A sunshine orange, kelly green, or a piercing violet isn't off-limits here. Go with your instincts and let the rest of the room follow suit. A bright color can be softened by different shades on chairs or a table, for example. Mixing in some touches of white can also provide a lightening effect. Pair stripes or polka dots in varying shades for a youthful look in fabrics and other elements, or even on the walls. Patterns can be just as much fun as a bright, solid color.

Whether bold and bright or soft and feminine, fantasy can mix with pragmatism if you keep practical needs in mind while adding decorative elements. The playroom is a highly trafficked area where kids want free reign; try to accommodate them accordingly. Stain-resistant fabrics, sturdy surfaces, and plenty of comfortable seating can be achieved stylishly, especially if you mix it up with bright colors, plush fabrics, and whimsical details.

LEFT Turn an unused nook into a unique playhouse. This cupboard on a stair landing was transformed into a fantastical play space with some climbing stairs and a lot of imagination.

ABOVE Transform plain, white columns into a wilderness fantasy with lifelike renderings of trees for a whimsical playroom. Cover floors with tiles for a surface where kids can play without restrictions.

KID-FRIENDLY: flooring

When it comes time to choose the padding for a playroom's floor, try to combine levity of style with durability and stain resistance. Kids should not only be allowed to be messy here, they also should feel as comfortable flopping down on the floor to read or play as sitting in one of the chairs. No rug burns are allowed!

Assess the needs of your room before making a decision. Is this a family room for relaxing and playing with toys, or will there be messy craft projects taking place? A room reserved for light play and relaxation should have a comfortable and soft rug. Plush, wall-to-wall carpeting is cozy for an indoor play space where little strenuous activity takes place. Soft throw rugs placed around the room will brighten it up and add a soft floor mat where kids can get comfortable. Although sisal, sea grass, and other tough, woven materials are ideal for withstanding dirt and stains in a living room area, they may not be as soft as wool pile or cotton rugs for little ones' hands and feet, especially when playing on the floor. Or, if an easy-to-clean, functional environment is what you and your kids are after, then try wood floors or water-sealed tiles from which spills of paint, glue, and paper scraps can be easily swept or wiped away.

Does your playroom need to suit many types of activities? A multipurpose room can have both a carpeted space for lounging and an uncovered floor surface for messier pursuits. Carpet most of the room and leave a bare-floored area for art projects, or use throw rugs on wood floors that can be cleared away when an unobstructed floor area is needed.

Rugs with patterns and fun designs can also add an interesting element to the floor and will hide dirt and stains better than plain rugs. The playroom is the place where whimsy is allowed. Graphic patterns in funky colors add an edge to a room with a modernist leaning, whereas embroidered, kid-friendly patterns lend a rustic air to a country-style home. Shop around for patterned children's rugs in designs that adults and children alike will enjoy in traditional rectangular shapes and sizes.

FLOOR PLANS

- Think durable, stain-resistant, yet comfortable when shopping for kid-friendly rugs.
- Use tile, linoleum, or wooden flooring in your crafts room; it will make cleanup much easier.
- Combine two types of flooring to accommodate a versatile playroom—tiles on one side and rugs on the other.
- Create a comfort zone with soft, plush carpeting.
- Colorful and wildly-patterned rugs work well in the playroom.

OPPOSITE An open floor plan that contains lots of separate spaces allows your family to enjoy time together, even while pursuing separate activities. The bright colors and the painting warm up the otherwise cool industrial space, and the bare floor leaves space for floor play.

craft room

Do you have an ultra-creative family on your hands? It's wonderful to provide them an outlet for their specialties, and there's no better way to do that than to create a play area where craft and other art supplies are readily accessible and are unlikely to stain or damage anything when in use. In a craft room, cleanup time can be minimized if sinks and sponges are nearby and plenty of labeled storage bins are available. Colored walls and whimsical details can still figure into the design, but avoid overly fragile decorations or furnishings. Surfaces should be bare, resilient, and washable. Tiled or linoleum flooring is best so that paint, crayons, pencils, and glue can't damage them. It's also important that the area is well lit—lots of windows with abundant natural light is ideal. (Although, if your windows face the south or create a glare, you may want to hang adjustable shades on them.)

Purchase some good, working furniture, too, but make sure that it isn't too precious. Plastic tables and chairs that are well made and thick enough can do the trick, though stainless-steel or wood furniture may last longer. A large surface area is a must in the craft room. A long or wide table where kids can spread out their canvases, markers, and scissors is an ideal working area. An old wooden work table can be made even more resilient by attaching linoleum or a thin sheet of metal like zinc to its top. Even a floor stocked with comfortable cushions on which elbows can be propped will do. Easels for a budding painter are a good choice for a craft room. If surfaces are paint resistant and you keep the room well stocked with newspapers, sponges, or paper towels for cleanup, painting mishaps shouldn't be a problem.

Keep the area organized with clear plastic drawers and shelves labeled for convenience. Deep shelves— or even flat file drawers if you have room—are ideal for storing or drying paintings. Kids should keep track of their own supplies and organize them so they know where everything is. Make sure that play spaces for young children have only childproof paints and nonhazardous glues and pastes, too. If you have any doubt about a particular supply, read the label before deciding whether it belongs in your child's craft room.

Once kids enter school, a well-equipped craft room can easily double as a prep space for their science projects and school crafts, but a craft room or an art space doesn't have to be reserved for children. Adults can exercise their creativity there, too. Even if you don't paint or sculpt, a craft room is an ideal place for sewing, making scrapbooks, wrapping presents, constructing models, or, if appropriate provisions are made for tools, woodworking projects as well. Just plan for storage if adult supplies need to be kept apart from children's craft supplies, and make sure the tables and chairs are comfortable for both adults and children.

Finally, why not put up some inspiration? Cover the walls with whatever inspires you—your own or your children's artwork, prints from a museum, or found objects—or put up a large bulletin board, and let the whole family pin it with all of the above, plus cards, photos, and whatever takes their fancy.

STYLE FILE: kids' artwork

Let children sow their creative seeds by giving them the license to create whatever they want in an arts-oriented playroom. Drawing is a relaxing way to wind down and to express complex emotions, no matter what your child's age. Let your children be proud of their creations, too. Hang their artwork up for the whole family and visiting guests to admire. You can frame favorite pieces in ready-made frames. A playroom can even be entirely decorated with only your children's artwork, if just dedicating one wall isn't enough. Watercolor paintings, for example, regardless of your child's skill level, have a beautiful, ethereal look that anyone can enjoy. You don't have to stick to paintings or one-dimensional drawings either. Ceramics, collages, popcorn strung on thread for Christmastime, or any other sort of crafts should find a welcome home here. Think of fun projects that encourage children to decorate their own environment. Painted-glass kits that let kids fashion their own ornaments or decorations can be bought for a rainy day, or a space can be reserved for painting a mural of their own design. Arts and crafts don't have to be costly, either. Found objects make some of the best canvases. Get old bowling pins from a bowling alley, and paint faces and costumes to make "pin people" that will add color and whimsy to the play room. Scraps of felt and unused cloth can be made into puppets, and can also be hung on walls for a decorative touch when not in use. The best way to decorate the playroom or crafts room is by giving kids ownership and letting their handiwork cover the walls, ledges, and bookcases. Not only do they enjoy seeing their work displayed, it also fits right in with the fun, informal aesthetic.

GET CRAFTY

- Get kids into the habit of drawing or painting for a creative and emotional outlet.
- Designate one wall in the playroom as the "art wall," reserved entirely for kids' paintings, or decorate the room entirely with framed favorites.
- Let kids paint a mural on a whole wall or just part of it.
- Decorate with ceramics, pottery, or other decorative objects made at school or at home.
- Plan ahead for a rainy day, and gather materials for art projects.

SHOPPING: tables and chairs

TABLES AND CHAIRS

Tables should withstand years of artwork and play. Placing a table in an unobtrusive corner leaves the center of the room open for activity. It should be sturdy, but not so clunky or heavy that it looks out of place in a playroom. Make sure it's large enough for children to spread out their work. If more temporary table space is needed, use folding card tables made of wood or aluminum that can be stowed away in a closet when not in use.

If the playroom will be used primarily by children, remember to shop with small people in mind. Tables should be low to the ground, and chairs should be sturdy and sized accordingly. Heavy-duty plastic tables and chairs with removable legs are wonderful, small-scale pieces that can be adjusted as kids grow. Beanbags and cubes are wonderfully adaptable to any shape, size, or form of person, but some companies also make child-size upholstered club chairs and rocking chairs. (Keep in mind that beanbag chairs can be dangerous for babies who can't yet lift themselves up.)

For outdoor furniture, note before you buy that the material should be able to withstand the elements. Teak will weather to a beautiful soft gray. Specially coated plastics and metals can stay outdoors without rusting. Look for children's furniture that's meant for indoor as well as outside use, and make sure the material is weather resistant.

SEATING

Because the playroom isn't as formal as the rest of the house, its furnishings can be more flexible. You can decorate it like any room meant for leisure-time use, with comfortable couches, chairs, and lamps for reading. Or you can be more even more informal and decorate the playroom with furniture that is functional but flexible—not disposable, but not investment pieces, either. You can forgo the traditional couch and armchairs and choose colorful beanbags, poufs, or fabric-covered squares. These make great and affordable seating and they withstand active play. What's more, they're also light and moveable enough for kids to clear away or move around the room when they need lots of space to accommodate guests for a sleepover party or afternoon play date. Large floor cushions or futon chairs can also be used for extra seating, adding a comfortable, laid-back touch. Iron-framed butterfly chairs are another option. You can buy different colors and fabrics, ranging from twills to buttery leathers for a more dressed-up approach. Also, look for great fabrics in original prints and patterns.

PLAYROOM PICKS

- Buy at least one table and a few chairs scaled for kids; adult sizes will feel enormous to them.
- Make sure playroom furniture is both practical and playful.
- For comfortable alternative seating, try cushions, beanbags, cubes, and the like.
- Pick sturdy materials like plastic, metal, and painted wood.
- When shopping for outdoor furniture, look for weather-resistant materials.
- Make sure table surfaces accommodate craft work and art projects.

backyard playhouse

Are your living quarters too small for a dedicated playroom? If you have a yard, an outdoor play area can be the answer. Not only does space expand exponentially, but the potential for inadvertent stains on furniture, floors, or walls is gone. You no longer need to patrol vigilantly for markers and paints. Bring on the mud and sand, instead. The only materials that may need concern now are the kids' clothes!

A paved area in the backyard can be used in many ways; it provides an even surface for furniture and a place to play with trucks or jacks on the ground without getting too dirty. A porch or patio with a ceiling is a perfect antidote. Otherwise, flat paving stones, bricks, or oversize cement tiles can also function as flooring for an outdoor play space.

OPPOSITE A solid-wood deck leaves lots of room for all kinds of activities. Sturdy plastic furniture withstands lots of wear and tear, and child-size chairs with ears add a great touch of whimsy. A grassy plot for sports will also get plenty of use.

ABOVE This picnic table provides an inviting spot for family meals alfresco. The bright flowers are welcoming, and the built-in cooking space makes food preparation a breeze.

Unlike the indoor playroom, not much is needed outside. Trade indoor furniture for weather-resistant tables and chairs, and transfer toys outdoors. If you have some comfortable chairs and a few small tables, you may find that on nice days the whole family will sit outside. A sturdy umbrella that won't blow over in a breeze is a bonus when the sun is hot. If you have a lawn and want to encourage the family to congregate there, consider investing in equipment for games like badminton, boccie, croquet, and even Frisbee golf. A sandbox or a swing set is ideal for outdoor play.

Find a place inside where furniture and toys can be stowed away when not in use, or make sure they can stand up to rain and snow. Outdoor storage units can be attractive, and they can also be camouflaged. Water-resistant covers can be bought for some outdoor furniture, or, if you have a covered porch, place furniture there—it will last longer. Even weather-resistant pieces can become discolored when out in the sun. Kids can play on a porch even during inclement weather or when you'd like them to stay out of the sun.

ORGANIZING: storage spaces

A playroom is often a converted garage or porch, or a transformed nook, and consequently doesn't always come outfitted with closets. If yours does, count yourself lucky for having a built-in storage space where toys, extra folding furniture, art supplies and tools, and other games can be stored. If your playroom doesn't have a closet, an arrangement of boxes, shelves, and other creative solutions can serve.

To keep toys and supplies under control, you'll need a lot of separate storage boxes or drawers. Objects like markers, crayons, blocks, toy cars, plastic farm animals, building toys, and many smaller items need storage boxes of their own because they become difficult to play with if they're mixed in with other toys in a large toy box. Kids can't use them if they can't find them. The boxes can be stacked on shelves with toys, video games, CDs, and books. You can also use clear-plastic bins for larger toys and stuffed animals so that when they aren't in use, they can still be clearly visible and easily found when wanted. Bookcases can also hold objects or boxes without obscuring them from sight.

For the playroom with lots of arts-and-crafts activity, a closet can help, but so can tabletop trays or bins to hold markers, pencils, scissors, paintbrushes, and messy paint tubes and jars. Markers or crayons can also be stashed in pencil cups, mason jars, or funky cans or boxes.

If there's a television, stereo, or video game system in the playroom, that means the accompanying videos, CDs, and game cartridges are also nearby. A video- or CD-storage unit nearby keeps these organized, as will bookshelves or a chest of drawers.

SUPPLY CLOSET

- Use plastic bins, drawers, and boxes to store larger items that you'd still like to keep visible.
- Store items in étagères, shelves, or bookcases for easy access.
- Organize smaller art supplies in trays, cups, and jars so that messy paints are stored separately.
- Label supplies so that kids know where they are.
- Keep CDs, videos, DVDs, and video games in storage units specifically designed to accommodate them.

OPPOSITE An enclosed patio space is great fun for toddlers to explore. The table with benches provides comfortable seating, and the statue livens up the space.

ROOM TO ROAM

PLAY AREAS INSIDE AND OUT

OFTEN, WHEN FAMILIES ARE GROWING and there is a mix of toddlers and young children in the home, toys, games, books, and art projects begin to spill into all rooms of the house. A dedicated playroom, if space permits, can not only help you keep things in check but also offer your children a place to play among themselves, or with friends in a room that totally serves their interests.

A playroom is not meant to segregate the children from family life; rather, it is a little piece of the home that caters to their needs, a place where they can play in a carefree setting. A playroom is a great place for children to gather after school or in inclement weather, and the perfect locale for completing an art project. When the children are old enough to comprehend their ownership of the room, they can begin to learn lessons in organization and how to keep the room tidy.

Likewise, outdoor play space is a wonderful way to get your children fresh air, sunshine, and exercise. It can teach them about nature and the outdoors, and keep them under your watchful eye.

This chapter is meant to inspire you on the possibilities of indoor and outdoor play spaces by illustrating a variety of solutions and design elements and showing you how to achieve them. These playrooms include inside rooms as well as backyard tree houses.

As you browse these pages, note how you might adapt a design, layout, and furnishing solutions to suit your family's needs. Creating playrooms can turn out to be family building or painting projects, depending on your interests, talents, and budget.

Left: Locate an indoor playroom near an outdoor play area, if possible. These railings are painted in bright, appealing colors to lead the way to fun. The rugs are the perfect dark gray to handle lots of traffic. Furnishings are simple and functional—a game table and soft beanbag chairs. An inviting little coat- and hatrack is beside the door.

Creative Solutions for Indoor Play Spaces

Where Do You Put a Playroom?

Ideally, a playroom is located within the range of adult supervision or earshot. Listening to the way your children play can teach you a lot about their personality and communication skills. If there is an emergency or a disagreement in which you need to intervene, being steps away helps. Beyond that, windows that let in the daylight and fresh air make the playroom—or any room—a pleasant place to be.

If space allows, segregate the noisier musical instruments from the playroom. In fact, if your children are all interested in music, consider turning a portion of your basement into a music room. Miles, a young boy featured in chapter three, keeps his drum set in his bedroom, which is located down the hall from the kitchen and den. His city condominium doesn't have a playroom, but when he plays his drums, his parents can be in the living room and still hear one another.

How Do You Organize It?

A playroom can house just about anything your children play with. Help them maximize its use by creating a layout that divides the room into compartments.

For example, split the room into a wet side and dry side. The wet side can hold paints, markers, clay, bubbles—anything that can spill or mark and stain the surroundings.

On the dry side, store the following:

- puzzles
- board games
- sports equipment
- dolls
- books
- television

- building blocks
- videotapes
- toys for playing make-believe including:
  - kitchen setup
  - doctor's bag,
  - fireman's outfit

Above: What could be more appropriate for the wet side of a room than a water theme? And who says the chairs have to match? Chairs in different styles and colors make this room more fun. Notice the sea creatures painted on them—a nice touch to carry the overall theme.

Opposite: Your children will likely love the same rooms you do! Windows that let in fresh air and sunshine are highly desirable; this room illustrates the point perfectly. Notice also the flooring—big, multicolored rubber puzzle pieces—great for little kids, who take the occasional spill. The room offers plenty of pint-sized seating and activities.

If possible, color code shelves and the containers that they house: a blue sticker on the "puzzle shelf" and matching stickers on the puzzle boxes can make clean up easy and fun for kids and their friends.

A bulletin board is a handy feature. Post your children's parties, sporting events, school outings, and birthdays of friends and teachers in view. Help the kids personalize the board and decorate it together.

Another good family project is making a crafts box for the playroom. Fill it with pipe cleaners, colorful yarn, buttons, glitter, and stickers for imaginative play.

If the room has no closet, it's a good idea to store a roll of paper towels—perhaps on a dispenser—near the paints and markers, and a dustpan tucked under a shelf or bookshelf.

Floors

Should you decide to divide the room into wet and dry sides, consider using linoleum tiles or vinyl that comes in sheets for the whole room. Then, for the dry side, or a portion thereof, add an area rug, which allows children to do puzzles or construct toy train tracks on a level, quiet surface.

Make the floor a major design element by choosing bright, colorful linoleum tiles and creating an interesting pattern or map of the room's specific areas. For example, designate yellow as the main color and use red tiles to lead to the paint and easel section, blue tiles to the television and video area, and green to the bookshelves. The colored tiles act like little roadways that stop at each area. Explore the possibility of having linoleum tiles custom-cut to interesting shapes. Center the wet area with a multicolored original art design your children first draw on paper.

Above: Consider these storage solutions. Paint a flea market table and cover the front with your favorite fabric to hide clumsy, odd-shaped items that won't store easily on shelves. Search flea markets for shelving you can revitalize. Alternatively, buy unfinished shelves and paint them yourself—or have your children apply their own designs.

Opposite: Tuck a shelving box here and there for great little cubbies. Save money by purchasing unfinished furniture, then paint to match the room. Carry the theme of the room to the wall by cutting out a template from stiff cardboard, pinning it to the wall, tracing it, then painting away!

To make the carpeted area more interesting, talk to a carpet showroom manager about buying strips cut from other installations. Create a visually interesting carpeted section by mixing tweeds with stripes and primary colors.

Remember, too, that the playroom need not be cut in half. Divide it any way that makes sense. Make a quarter of the room a reading or quiet corner; install carpet in that area only. Another option is to paint a hardwood floor with a fun color, with a pattern of diamonds or stars, or with words that suggest activities for each area.

Walls

To save cleaning time and trouble, explore the following wallcover possibilities:

- **Blackboard paint:** Cover an entire wall, all four walls, a slice of wall, or the bottom half of all the walls in the room with blackboard paint, and give your children the freedom to express themselves.
- **Semigloss latex paint:** This is good for all the places little hands go—doors, window frames, and walls. A soapy sponge or window cleaner cleans this paint well.
- **Washable wallpaper:** Install this paper all around, or paint on the lower half and install wallpaper on top.

If your budget allows, hire an art student or a painter to create a cheery, interesting mural for the children to look at. This could work especially well if your playroom has no windows or poor light.

Above: There's no need to worry about fingerprints or sticky hands when walls are washable. Use semigloss paint or washable wallpaper. And do have fun! This bright red room, with clowns, big wooden farm animals, and painted furniture, would make any child feel welcome and happy.

Above: To brighten a room with too few windows, consider painting a scene on the walls. This works like wallpaper that tells a story and gives you and your child ideas to talk about. Note the padded toy box, great for little ones who could slam a finger or bump into the box.

Above: Even toddlers need a place to be creative, and in this room with kitties, flowers, and puppies on the fabric and wallpaper, it's easy to be artistically inspired!

Furniture

When children are playing they move furniture and things around to suit their activities, so the lighter the better for playroom furnishings. Good choices include wicker, plastic, and air-filled furniture. Choose a style that fits the age group, and certainly consider bringing in that old sofa you were going to give away. Cover it with brightly colored sheets and let the children climb on it and play. If snacks or soda spill, you won't fret.

Another option is to buy big pillows and spread a few around the room.

Here's a list of playroom furniture to consider:

- child size chairs
- crafts table
- easel
- storage crates or baskets
- oversize pillows

Children love to play in enclosures, so, if you can, devote a portion of the room to a tent. Purchase a lightweight nylon tent from a camping store—it can be used both inside and outside—or fashion a simple tent from fabric. Some children's catalogs offer play tents, as well as flexible nylon crawl-through tubes and cardboard houses that can be colored with markers. Look through catalogs for playful ideas you might adapt and craft yourself.

Above: Here is a cheery playroom for toddlers. The lime-green painted wood, sunny papered walls, and the animal theme, from the curtains to the wall art, sets a fun mood.

Opposite: Children's outdoor play spaces can be as simple or elaborate as you wish. This amazing replica of a real house shows that our imagination, carpentry talents, time, and budget are our only limits!

Window Treatments

Keep window treatments simple and select easy-to-care-for solutions. If you want the ability to darken the room, shades are a good choice. Cover them with wallpaper or fabric that matches the room, or have a painting party with acrylics, and allow each of your children to design a shade. Another good option, if you sew, is to make café curtains to match a colorful fabric sheet you throw over the couch. If one side of the playroom is for paints, use vinyl curtains that would ordinarily be used in a child's bath.

If the room does not face the street, the children can make their own window decorations. For example, they could put a drawing in the bottom half of each window or paint a picture right on the glass (with the right paint, of course). They can use windowsills as display areas for their clay creations.

Outside Spaces

Finding Equipment

Many prefabricated exercise and play areas are available for backyard fun, as are tree house plans. An excellent way to research these is on the Internet, where you can view equipment and plans and correspond with the companies or, in some cases, with the actual designers. Search with your favorite search engine or library computer and look for the words "tree house" or "gym equipment" for a vast array of information. To check on the safest choices, do plenty of research, contact consumer safety groups, and consult parenting magazines before making the investment.

SITING A **PLAY AREA**

Kids love to be outdoors, pushing trucks through the sand or swinging high into the air. If you're going to have an outdoor swing set or sandbox, it's probably a good idea to site it under the shade of a tree to keep your children from the intense summer sun. This won't take the place of lotions, but it will help.

For toy storage, consider spray-painting a vinyl garbage bin bright red or yellow and placing it outside the back door. Make sure to buy one that your children can reach into easily. The bin will protect metal toys from rusting and keep other toys out of the elements as well.

As for the tree house, select a healthy tree with a good branch configuration to hold the structure. Height placement and access rights depend on the ages of your children.

Look for a level section of land in your yard, one that has good drainage as well. You don't want your sandbox sitting in a pool of soggy grass after a rainstorm.

Construct or buy a sandbox, or build a mock sandbox by edging a desired area with brick or a low metal sheet then fill that area with beach sand. Be careful if there are cats in the neighborhood; the sand will remind them of a litter box. If you do have cats nearby, a covered or gated sandbox will work best.

FURNISHING A **TREE HOUSE**

A tree house can provide a great escape and learning experience for kids. It gives them a space they can feel ownership over, and a tree house can teach them some of the responsibilities of adulthood—like keeping it clean. It can also encourage creativity, as the children can imagine the tree house as a remote castle or a secret hideaway. Read on for tips to make it feel a little more hospitable:

Simple ideas to decorate a tree house:

Cover old pillows or dog beds with washable fabric, and use as seats.

Make curtains from old sheets, blankets, towels, or pillowcases. Turn a hem, and for rods, use long sticks that rest on large cup rings and screw into the wall.

Have an art day when your children decorate. Use leftover wallpaper, paint, or floor tiles, and see how your kids integrate them here.

Cover the walls with snapshots of their friends or attach to a bulletin board you've hung here.

Try glow-in-the-dark stars or glow-in-the-dark paint on the ceiling.

To keep out mosquitoes, buy screen on a roll and staple it to the window frame. To liven things up, consider spray-painting the screen a fun color, and attaching paper bugs for atmosphere!

What can you put in a tree house? Here are a few suggestions your children may enjoy:

• an old blanket

• a board game or two that won't suffer in moisture

• a tin of hard candies

• a picnic basket for summertime lunches

• a disposable camera

• drawing supplies

• a plastic box for a few books and magazines

• suntan lotion

• bubble solution

• inexpensive binoculars and a bird book

• a butterfly net

• a flashlight

• bug repellent

• a guidebook to the planets and stars

• an inexpensive telescope

PET PLACES

If you have a dog or cat, or plan to, designing places for them to sit or perch is a good idea, as is thinking about the reality of their habits. Discuss with your children where the pet is allowed in your home, and how to best accommodate. In addition, you can design places for leashes, food, toys, and even litter storage, so that your children can participate in their care. Here are a few tips:

For the Dog

If you have a mudroom, or back door that your children frequently use to go outside with the pup, put a peg or hook for the leash at their height for easy access. In addition, consider adding a peg or hook that holds a vinyl bag for balls, and other dog toys. If there's room, add a third peg for a bag of edible treats.

Family dogs typically like to be with the family, and this usually means on the rug—not the easy-to-clean uncarpeted floor. If you leave the house, most often they sit and wait for you by the door. Consider placing a dark, richly patterned rug that won't show the hair or occasional wet paws. Or, put an extra bed there, over the rug; choose a fabric cover that complements the theme of the entry.

An option for dog food storage is a wicker hamper or closed wicker box that fits under an open counter at child height, or fits in the hall outside the kitchen. Or, you can create a family art project, and paint a wooden box—collage it with photos of your pet—and store in your kitchen. Do the same for treats!

When dogs come in from the rain, or snow, they need to be dried off. Make that your children's responsibility. Keep small, absorbent towels in the doorway in either a box or in a colorful pillowcase that you've strung with twine and hung on a peg.

Look around your house and see where else the dog tends to hang out, and add either a rich-colored, washable rug or another bed. Make your own pet bed cover to match the room or area, or put down a washable throw.

Cats

More than one pet owner holds the theory that the cat owns the house and simply allows the humans to visit. But, even though kitties go wherever they want to, you can make things that are helpful in cutting down on pet hair.

The simplest, and most attractive, is the common wicker basket lined with an old towel or blanket. Place one where the sun shines.

Ask your children to help you make the area even more attractive by selecting pretty fabric and crafting a simple cover for an old pillow. Try weaving ribbon in and out of the basket, or painting the outside in a cheerful hue that blends with the space.

If you notice, cats also like beds, or your favorite chair. Hem a pretty piece of fabric (with hem tape!), and place it on those spots to contain fur.

The food area—often a messy place—is another opportunity for kid-made crafts for pets: decorate a special placemat or two and use it to keep the feeding area tidy.

 If windows do not exist in number or at a height that accommodates a seat, hang a painting that depicts a window and outdoor scene. Alternatively, paint such a scene directly on the wall. Put a reading chair and bookshelf against it.

Instead of building a window seat, purchase a toy box or chest, cover it with a cushion, and place it in front of a window.

DECORATING TIPS FROM THE KIDS

Aram

When 7-year-old Aram was asked to draw his favorite thing in his room, he drew his younger brother, Van. Asked what he would love to have in his room, he drew a window seat, and tossed in some books to illustrate what he would do there.

If his parents chose to construct a window seat because it would look good and worked with a redesign budget they had, perfect. Window seats, constructed as simple boxes that open, add storage and seating. A number of examples are shown in Chapter 3.

Tommine

When Tommine's mom told her about my interest in having her draw her dream room, she took it as a special assignment. The 8½-year-old came to my house with detailed sketches in hand, prepared to color them while I watched. I quickly saw how much she wanted to communicate clearly what she loved. I couldn't help but smile at this trendy retro room.

Clearly, between 8 and 10, children begin to register fads and want to embrace them everywhere. The transition presages the jumps from 10 to 12 and 14 to 16, when individuality dramatically prevails! Consider how to anticipate these changes while accommodating present tastes.

Review these suggestions on working today's design preferences into a room while allowing convenient modification when the next trend hits:

- Cover the upper half of the walls with a bulletin board. Suggest that your child draw big illustrations of favorite things and pin them up.

- Paint the lower half of the wall a trendy color. This limits your investment to a gallon of purple paint, which can be inexpensively covered with the next popular shade.

- Buy unfinished furniture that can be painted and repainted quickly to accommodate changing tastes.

- Explore catalogs for moderately priced, trendy scatter rugs and bedcovers. The flower rug and smiley face are easy to find.

AT COOPER'S HOUSE

When Ann was pregnant with Cooper, she thought she would need to move her numerous collections—everything from birds' eggs to antique toys—to the safety of the attic of her dreamy 1800s sea captain's house. She was partially correct.

In fact, before Cooper became a toddler, the collections comprised objects
Ann and her husband, Chris, could
point to and amuse, teach, or distract
him with. The breakfast room, for example, is accented with bright colors
and houses eggs and butterflies. Likewise, the bathroom on the second
floor features a wicker chair full of
seashells.

Now that Cooper can walk, some collections were moved to the attic for
protection. To protect Cooper himself,
gates were installed at the top and bot
tom of the stairs. The glass bookcase
that held a collection of tin toys was retired to the attic; if Cooper pulled its
knobs, the whole thing could crash.
Chris advises parents to lay carpeting
everywhere they can and install gates
to avoid the injuries that come with
inevitable falls.

Cooper's walker and swing bore him
now now that he is walking. For his
protection, sharp corners in the
kitchen are padded. Thresholds may
still trip him as he meanders from
room to room, but he is proving more
coordinated than Ann expected.

The distinctive decor—shabby chic
and flea market finds—along with
Chris' bad art collection, continues to

stimulate Cooper as he walks. The fuss-free environment means he can play wherever he wishes. Perhaps there is a lesson here for all parents: Sprinkle colorful objects throughout your home as stimulating distractions for baby.

The original design idea for Cooper's bedroom was a cowboy or pirate theme, but his parents worried this was antiquated. Plain and colorful won out. Perhaps when he turns four, the room will be redone to reflect his developing interests and personality.

The walls are hand-painted by Ann, who traced a diamond grid all around the room. Cooper's crib is new, as are his dresser and bookcase. They were purchased unfinished and painted as well. Ann worried about lead paint, so she opted for painting everything herself. She might have been more apt to go for antique or flea market pieces normally, but she did not want to strip furniture while pregnant.

Ann did introduce one flea market find—an old rocker—recovering the seat pillow with Ralph Lauren fabric. The changing table, so temporary in a baby's life, was borrowed from a neighbor.

The bedroom's lack of closets called for some construction. Ann's father extended the wall at either side of the changing table and added closet doors. He put shelving and two rods in each, one for Cooper when he can hang his clothes and one at adult height.

When Cooper is older, he may graduate to the guest room across the hall, which is twice as big. Both rooms are near his parents'.

The bright yellow furnishings are cheery and provide a pleasing contrast to the soft colors of the diamonds. The lime-green curtains are made from bedsheets. The wall-to-wall carpeting is inexpensive; it was chosen to disappear into the decor. Its value is in function and safety.

MATERIALS

Canvas floor cloth, 2' x 3'
(.6 m x .9 m)

Masking tape

Ruler

Chalkboard finish, green

Expandable sponges, pack of 5

Scissors

Small plastic containers

Acrylic paints, Red, Blue, Yellow

Waxed paper

Sticky-back black felt squares

Chalk

OPTION: TIC-TAC-TOE PIECES

Polymer modeling clay,
two 2 oz. packages of each:
red, yellow, blue, green, and white

Glass baking dish

CHALKBOARD ROLL-UP

A perfect tool for a child's room or playroom with limited space, this chalkboard is perfect for drawing and practicing letters and numbers, or for special messages and great for car travel, too! Hang it on a wall or lay it on the floor. When you're finished, simply roll it up to store in a closet. Spray Chalkboard Finish makes this project possible. Simply spray the finish on a canvas floor cloth to create a fully erasable chalkboard surface. Then embellish your design with sponge-painted shapes. Materials make one chalkboard and one eraser. Double your fun by making polymer clay Xs and Os for hours of tic-tac-toe fun with your new chalkboard.

INSTRUCTIONS

1. Unroll the floor cloth and tape it down to a flat surface in a well-ventilated area. Use masking tape to mask off the area to be sprayed. Measure 3.5" (9 cm) in from each 2' (.6 m) side of the floor cloth, and tape a straight line (parallel to the edge of the canvas) to form the short sides of the rectangle. Then mask a random zig-zag design on each long side of the rectangle. Spray the Chalkboard Finish in several thin coats to avoid drips and puddles. Let dry, then remove the masking tape.

2. Trace simple shapes, such as stars, Xs, and Os, onto the compressed sponges. Cut out with scissors. Expand the sponges by running them under water, then let dry slightly. Mix paint colors in the small containers: yellow and blue for green; yellow and red for orange; and red and blue for purple. Spread some of all six colors (red, blue, yellow, green, orange and purple) onto waxed paper, and dip the sponge shapes into the paint. Wipe off any excess paint before stamping the shapes onto the border. Alternate and overlap your shapes to decorate the whole border.

3. Cut the self-stick felt into 12 equal pieces measuring 2" x 4.5" (5 cm x 11 cm). Put 2 pieces together (sticky side to sticky side) to create the bottom of the eraser. Then stack 9 more pieces (sticky side down) squarely on top of the original two. Cut the remaining 2" x 4.5" (5 cm x 11 cm) piece in half lengthwise, then trim 1" (3 cm) off of each end of one of those pieces. You will have one 1" x 4.5" (3 cm x 11 cm) piece and one 1" x 2.5" (3 cm x 6 cm) piece. Center the shorter piece on top of the longer piece, sticky side to sticky side. Then stick this new piece sticky side down to the top of the eraser, forming a handle.

OPTION: TIC-TAC-TOE PIECES

Instructions

1. For each O piece, take $\frac{1}{4}$ block of green clay, $\frac{1}{4}$ block of blue clay, and $\frac{1}{8}$ block of white clay, and shape each into a short, fat, worm shape. Lay all three worms next to each other lengthwise. Twist the three worms together as the clay stretches. Fold the twisted worm in half and twist until you achieve a marbleized look. Shape the worm into an O.

2. To make an X, repeat the marbleizing process with $\frac{1}{4}$ block of yellow clay, $\frac{1}{4}$ block of red clay, and $\frac{1}{8}$ block of white clay. When you have made your red, yellow, and white worm, form the worm into an X. Make six of each shape and bake them according to package directions.

TIPS

• Spray paint travels, so cover anything in the immediate area around the canvas. Read the directions on the can before spraying paint.

• When cutting out shapes from the sponge, use a craft knife to help cut out the center of the O.

• Save the sponge shapes for future art and crafts projects, or use them to decorate a playroom wall.

MATERIALS

Unfinished wooden stool,
14" x 10" x 11.5"
(36 cm x 25 cm x 29 cm)

Wood filler

Fine sandpaper

Paintbrush 1" (3 cm)

Acrylic paint, white

Stencil patterns (see pgs. 264–265)

Glue

Lightweight cardboard

Craft knife

Colored pencils: orange,
magenta, turquoise,
green, yellow

Acrylic spray sealer, matte

Pencil sharpener

FUNKY FISH STOOL

This useful footstool combines a simple geometric design with the fish pattern of your choice. Keep this stool near the sink for little ones to wash up or in the playroom to reach books and games on the upper shelves. Keep your pencils sharp and your stencils lined up, and you can produce this decorated footstool in a day! Simply paint the stool white. Then, use the patterns provided to make your own stencils from cardboard. Use your child's drawings to create your own design. Substitute elements of your child's artwork for the patterns to create stencils that include the images he prefers. This is a good place to use his color choices, too, no matter how wild.

INSTRUCTIONS

1. Fill any nail holes with wood filler, and let the filler dry. Lightly sand any rough spots and filled-in areas so that all the surfaces are smooth.

2. Slightly thin a small quantity of white paint with water. Paint this as a primer coat on the stool. Let it dry, and sand lightly all over. Apply a second coat of white paint, straight from the bottle, and let dry. If necessary, sand the second coat and apply a third coat.

3. Using the stencil patterns, glue them to lightweight cardboard, and cut out the designs using a craft knife. Place the triangle shapes along the edge of the top of the stool. Using a loose sketching motion, fill in the shapes with colored pencils: orange on the left, magenta on the right, and turquoise in the corners of the stool. Stencil a green circle above the turquoise corners. Following the photo, color in the fish stencil. Using the yellow pencil, color in circles in a random pattern on each side of the stool. Color in the hook and fly on the crosspiece.

4. Spray a light coat of acrylic sealer over the entire stool. After the first coat dries completely, spray several more light coats, allowing each coat to dry between applications.

TIP

• Be careful not to spray the sealer too heavily as this may cause dripping and the colors to run.

Photocopy at 154%

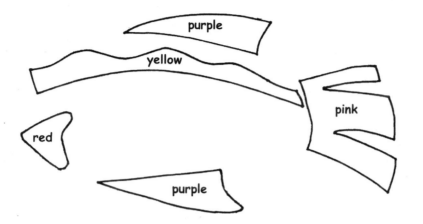

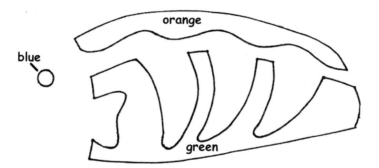

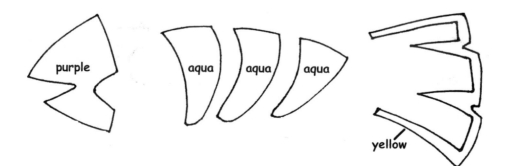

top of stool

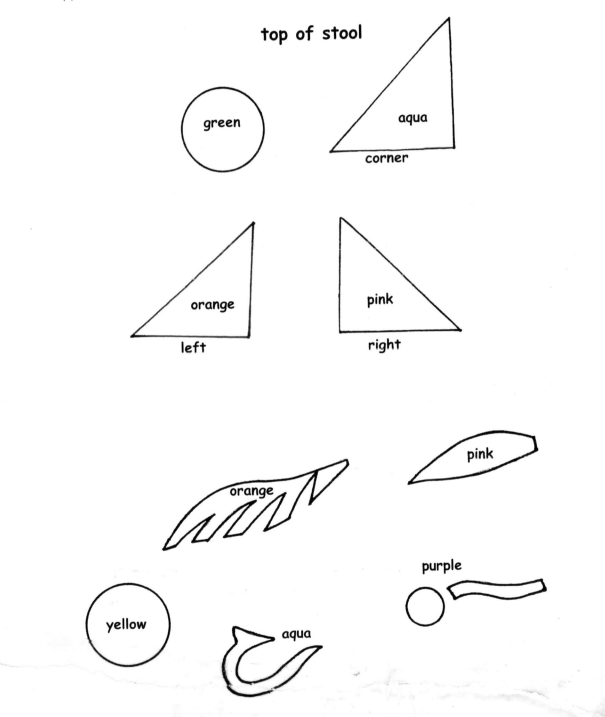

green

aqua

corner

orange

left

pink

right

orange

pink

yellow

aqua

purple

Resources

APPLIANCES

Sub-Zero
www.subzero.com
  Refrigerators, freezers, ice makers, wine storage

Viking
888-VIKING1
www.vikingrange.com
  Refrigerators, freezers, ice makers, wine storage

FABRICS

Anna French Fabrics Ltd.
(exclusive US retailer)
(617) 574-9030
  Fabrics and trimmings

Anna French Fabrics Ltd.
02077379640
  Fabrics and trimmings

Laura Ashley, Inc.
Phone (617) 457-6425
  Fabrics and trimmings

Beacon Hill
(800) 343-1470
  Fabrics and trimmings; to the trade only

Clarence House
(800) 221-4704
  Fabrics and wall coverings including velvets,
  damasks, silks, cottons, linens, sheers, trimmings,
  and leathers

Cowtan & Tout
(212) 647-6900
  Several lines of fabric; to the trade only

Country Swedish
www.countryswedish.com
  Classic quality furniture, fabrics, wallpapers, rugs,
  and other accessories designed and manufactured in
  Sweden; to the trade only

F. Schumacher
(800) 332-3384
  To the trade only

Heal's
20 7636 1666
www.heals.co.uk
  Fabrics, furniture, lighting, accessories

Kravet
(800) 645-9068
  Furniture, fabric, trimmings; to the trade only

Lee Jofa
(800) 453-3563
www.leejofa.com
  To the trade only

Osborne & Little
(212) 751-3333 for showrooms
  Fabrics and wallpapers with youthful patterns and
  colors; to the trade only

Marimekko
www.marimekko.fi
  Fabric and accessories; to the trade only

Ralph Lauren Home
(888) 475-7674
www.rlhome.polo.com

Shabby Chic
(310) 394-1975 or (212) 274-9842
  Slipcovered, easy-to-maintain upholstered
  furniture and fabrics

Silk Trading Co.
(800) 854-0396
www.silktrading.com
  Silk fabrics and ready-made curtains, bags

Summer Hill Ltd.
(650) 363-2600 for showrooms
  To the trade only

FIXTURES

Czech & Speake
800 5678 1234
British-based kitchen and bathroom fixtures, scents, and leather goods

Dornbracht
(800) 774-1181
Fixtures, fittings, bathroom accessories

Kallista
888-4-KALLISTA
www.killistainc.com

Kohler
(800) 4-KOHLER
www.kohler.com

Waterworks
(800) 899-6757
Fixtures, floorings, and bath accessories

FLOORING

Ann Sacks
(800) 278-8453
www.annsacks.com
Tiles

Armstrong Flooring
www.armstrong.com

Bisazza
(305) 597-4099
Glass tiles

DuPont Corian
(800) 4-CORIAN
www.corian.com
Solid surfacing in a range of color options

Home Depot
(770) 433-8211
www.homedepot.com
Home improvement store featuring flooring, hardware, accessories, supplies

Mirage Flooring
(800) 463-1303
Wood flooring

Walker Zanger
(877) 611-0199
www.walkerzanger.com
Tiles in ceramic, glass, metal, stone, and terra cotta

FURNITURE

Baker
(800) 59-BAKER
www.bakerfurniture.com
Luxe furniture

Crate & Barrel
(800) 996-9960
www.crateandbarrel.com
Furniture; featuring the Land of Nod for playroom, nursery, bedroom, and bathroom furniture for kids

Ethan Allen
(800) 228-9229
www.ethanallen.com
Furniture and upholstery, in-store decorating advisers

IKEA
www.ikea.com
Furniture, rugs, window treatments

John Lewis
20 7269 7711
www.johnlewis.co.uk
Furniture, lighting, fabrics, accessories

The Land of Nod
(800) 993-9904
www.landofnod.com

Maine Cottage
(207) 846-1430
www.mainecottage.com
Painted wood furniture

The Mitchell Gold Co.
www.mitchellgold.com
Upholstered furniture, child-sized armchairs and rocking chairs in a range of fabrics and slipcovers

PoshTots.com
www.poshtots.com
(866) POSH-TOTS
Features everything from convertible sleigh cribs to child-sized, painted armoires

Pottery Barn Kids
(800) 993-4923
  Furniture, rugs, linens, and more
  in kid-friendly shades and sizes

Ralph Lauren Home
(800) 475-7674
www.rlhome.polo.com
  Upscale furniture and accessories

Restoration Hardware
(800) 762-1005
www.restorationhardware.com
  Furniture, fixtures, accessories

Selfridges
20 629 1234
www.selfridges.com
  Furniture, lighting, fabrics, accessories

Shabby Chic
(310) 394-1975 or (212) 274-9842
  Slipcovered, easy-to-maintain
  upholstered furniture, fabrics

Smith & Hawken
(800) 940-1170
  Outdoor furniture, accessories

Urban Outfitters
(800) 282-2200
www.urbanoutfitters.com
  Beanbags, butterfly chairs, futons,
  playroom furniture

West Elm
(866) 841-7223
  Refined natural wood and fabric furniture

PAINT

Benjamin Moore
  www.benjaminmoore.com for store locator

Farrow and Ball
(888) 511-1121
www.farrow-ball.com
  British manufacturer

The Glidden Company
(800) 221-4100
www.gliddenpaints.com

Pratt & Lambert
(800) BUY-PRAT
www.prattandlambert.com

Sherwin-Williams
www.sherwinwilliams.com

STORAGE

California Closets
(888) 336-9709
www.calclosets.com
  Closet hardware, storage, and accessories

The Container Store
(888) CONTAIN
www.containerstore.com
  Storage and shelving for office, kitchen,
  laundry, and bathroom

Hold Everything
(800) 421-2264
www.holdeverything.com
  Storage solutions; home office furniture;
  bath, closet, and laundry accessories

Martha Stewart—The Catalog for Living
(800) 950-7130
www.marthastewart.com
  Storage accessories, furniture, bedding, and more

Target
(800) 800-8800
www.target.com
  Furniture, one-stop shopping for organizing
  laundry, kitchen, shelving, and clothing

CATALOGS

These are catalogs I have personally gone through and receive regularly. All of them have items that will help you decorate. Please note that not all are specifically aimed at children, but you will find items appropriate for children's and family rooms.

Call these numbers to receive a catalog, or visit the websites.

Anthropologie
(800) 543-1039
www.anthropologie.com

Charles Keath
(800) 388-6565
www.charleskeath.com

estyle.com/babystyle.com/kidstyle.com
(877) 378-9537

Garnet Hill
(800) 622-6216

L'Art de Vivre
(800) 411-6515
www.indulge.com

Linensource
(800) 431-2620
www.linensource.com

Martha by Mail
(800) 950-7130
www.marthabymail.com

The Nature Company
(800) 227-1114

Neiman Marcus
(800) 825-8000
www.neimanmarcus.com

Pottery Barn
(800) 922-9934 or (800) 922-5507

Shades of Light
(800) 262-6612

Sundance
(800) 422-2770
www.sundancecatalog.com

Windoware
(800) 248-8888

WEBSITES FOR CHILDREN'S ITEMS

You can see hundreds, maybe thousands of items, from cribs to desks to lamps, at any of these websites. Precede addresses with www.

allwoodusa.com

amishmall.net

armsreach.com

babycyberstore.com

babygear.com

babyproductsonline.com

babystyle.com

bellini.com

bizrate.com

bunnies.com

calendarexpress.com

childwoodproducts.com

cozycreations.com

find-furniture.com

fingerhut.com

furniturechannel.com

furniturefan.com
  (Use this site to search stores by zip code and product.)

grant.ent.com

guild.com

homeportfolio.com

iwillsave.com

kidcarpet.com

kidstation.com

kidstyle.com

littlebobbycreations.com

momastore.org

niftycool.com

productnetwork.com

ross-simons-online.com

seebuy.com

stores.suncommerce.com

storesearch.com

toyboxesetc.com

tuffyland.com

uniquehomegifts.com

Photographer Credits

Peter Aprahamian, Living Etc./IPC Syndication, 84

Courtesy of Armstrong Flooring, 16; 108-109

Courtesy of Laura Ashley Ltd., 29 (left); 63; 66; 87 (bottom)

Andrew Bordwin, 28; 29 (right); 167; 168; 173; 175 (inset)

Courtesy of California Closets, 11; 131; 146; 147; 150; 202

Courtesy of Craftopia.com, 48; 50; 96-103; 190-192; 260–265

Carlos Domenech, 110

Tim Ebert, 38; 88

Anna French Ltd., 26; 34; 35 (bottom); 39 (top); 62; 65; 71; 87 (top); 89 (bottom); 177 (bottom); 179 (top); 181; 244; 246; 249 (top); 252

Tria Giovan, 155

Courtesy of The Glidden Company, 15; 68; 143; 149; 163; 195

John Hall, 179 (bottom); 239

Courtesy of Ikea, 125; 153; 207; 210

Tim Imrie/Family Circle/IPC Syndication, 175

Peter Jacquith/Junior League of Boston Showhouse, 31

Peter Jacquith/Pam Mazow, Design, 208

Anna Kasabian, 41; 42; 91; 254

Nancy Klemm, 43; 90; 185; 189; 255

Sandy Levy, Courtesy of Terry Tiles, 182; 183

Deborah Whitlaw Llewellyn, 12; 73; 78; 136; 215 (left); 223; 123

John Edward Linden/Avanti Architects, 221

John Edward Linden/Tom Carson Architects, 226

John Edward Linden/Fernau & Hartman, Architects, 79; 233

Ray Main/www.mainstreamimages.co.uk, 142; 217

Courtesy of Maine Cottage Furniture, 112; 120; 145; 199; 205; 231

Richard Mandelkorn, 176

Courtesy of Marimekko, 218

Paul Massey/Living Etc./IPC Syndication, 72; 119; 135; 137; 160; 161; 204; 234; 144

B. Miebach/Jahreszeiten Verlag, 32

Keith Scott Morton, 75

About the Authors

ANNA KASABIAN is the author of eight books; her most recent title is *New England Style*. She writes about food, interior design, garden crafts, and home and garden preservation projects. Her freelance work appears *Yankee, Country Living, Coastal Living, Country Living Gardener,* and *Kitchen & Cook,* among other national magazines. She has been featured on HGTV and National Public Radio's Boston affiliate, WBUR. She also writes for OldHouseWeb.com.

Writer and design specialist EUGENIA SANTIESTEBAN currently serves as assistant editor for *Elle Décor*.